BLOOM Coloring Book

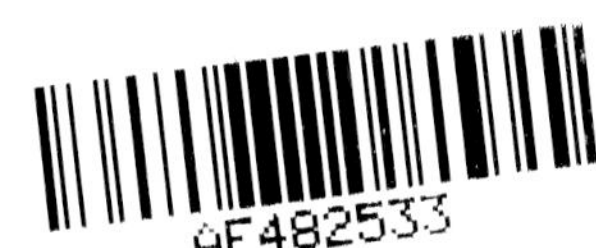

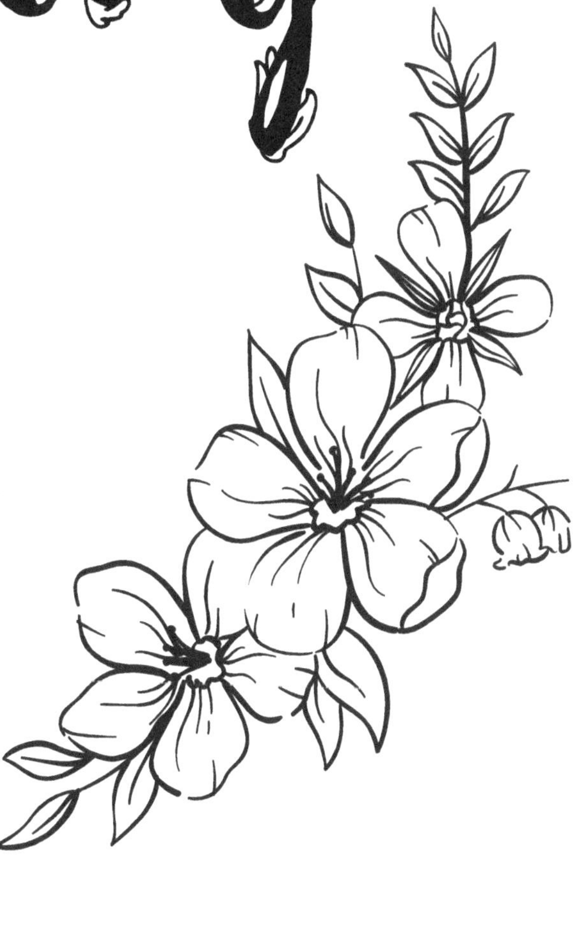

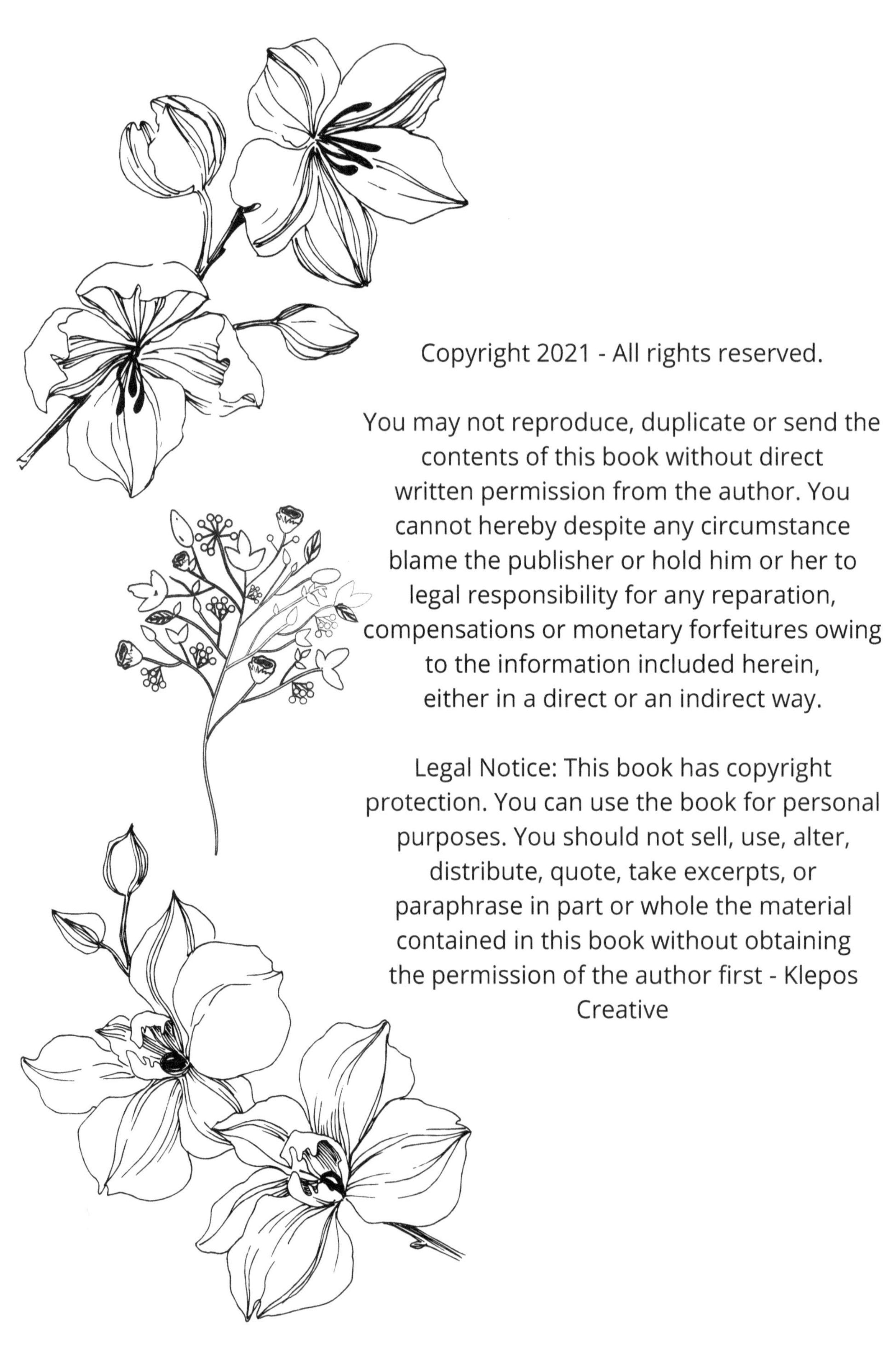

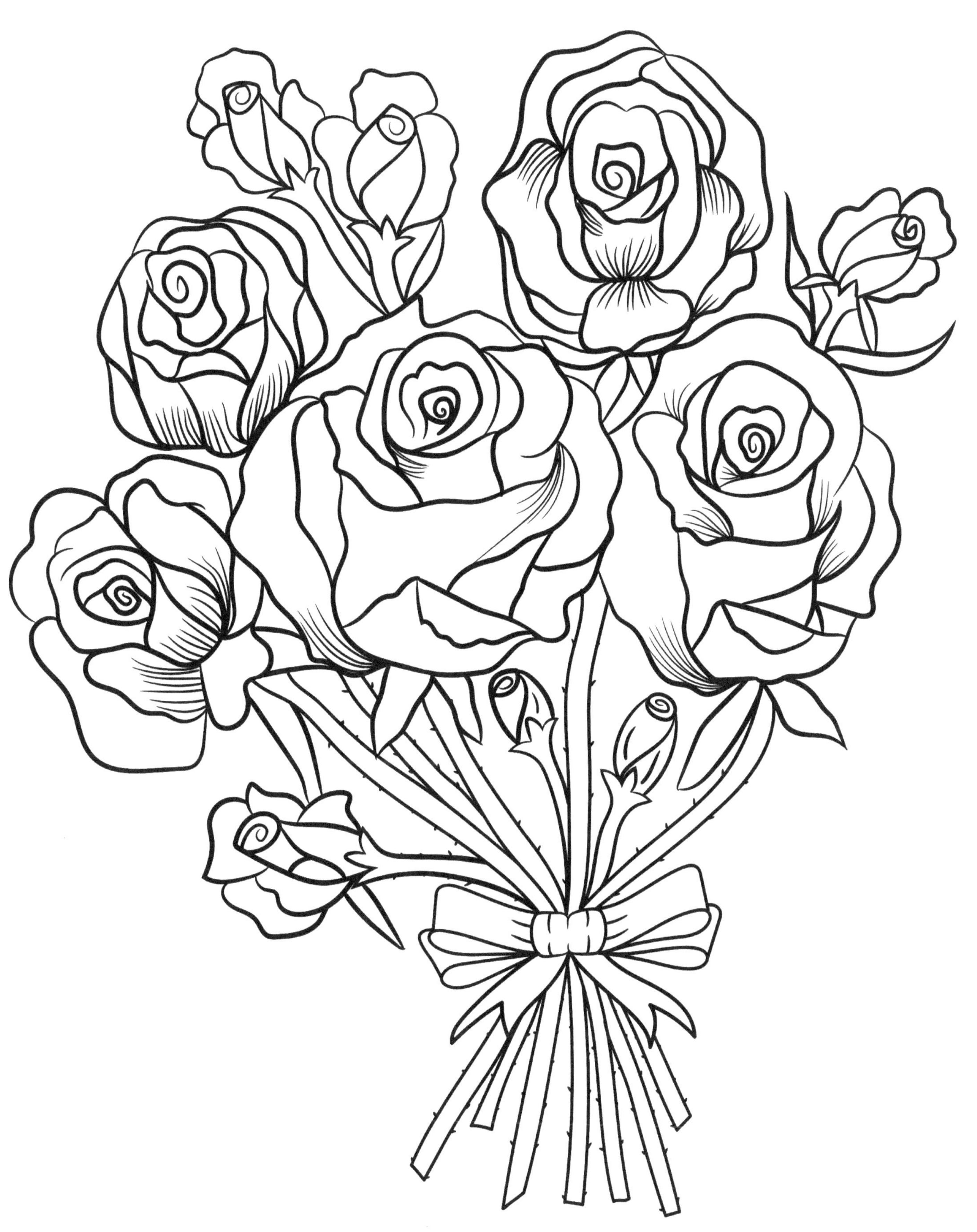

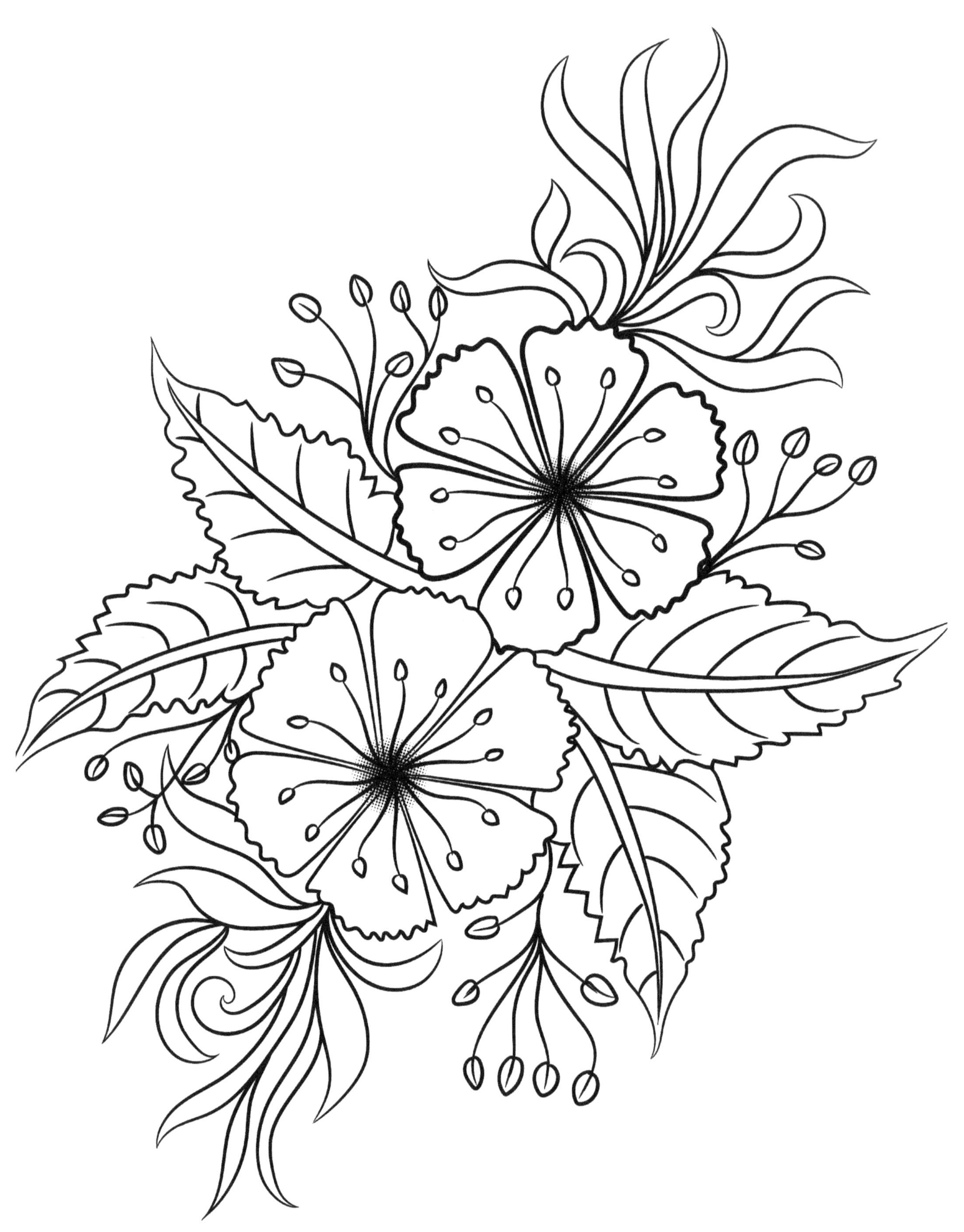

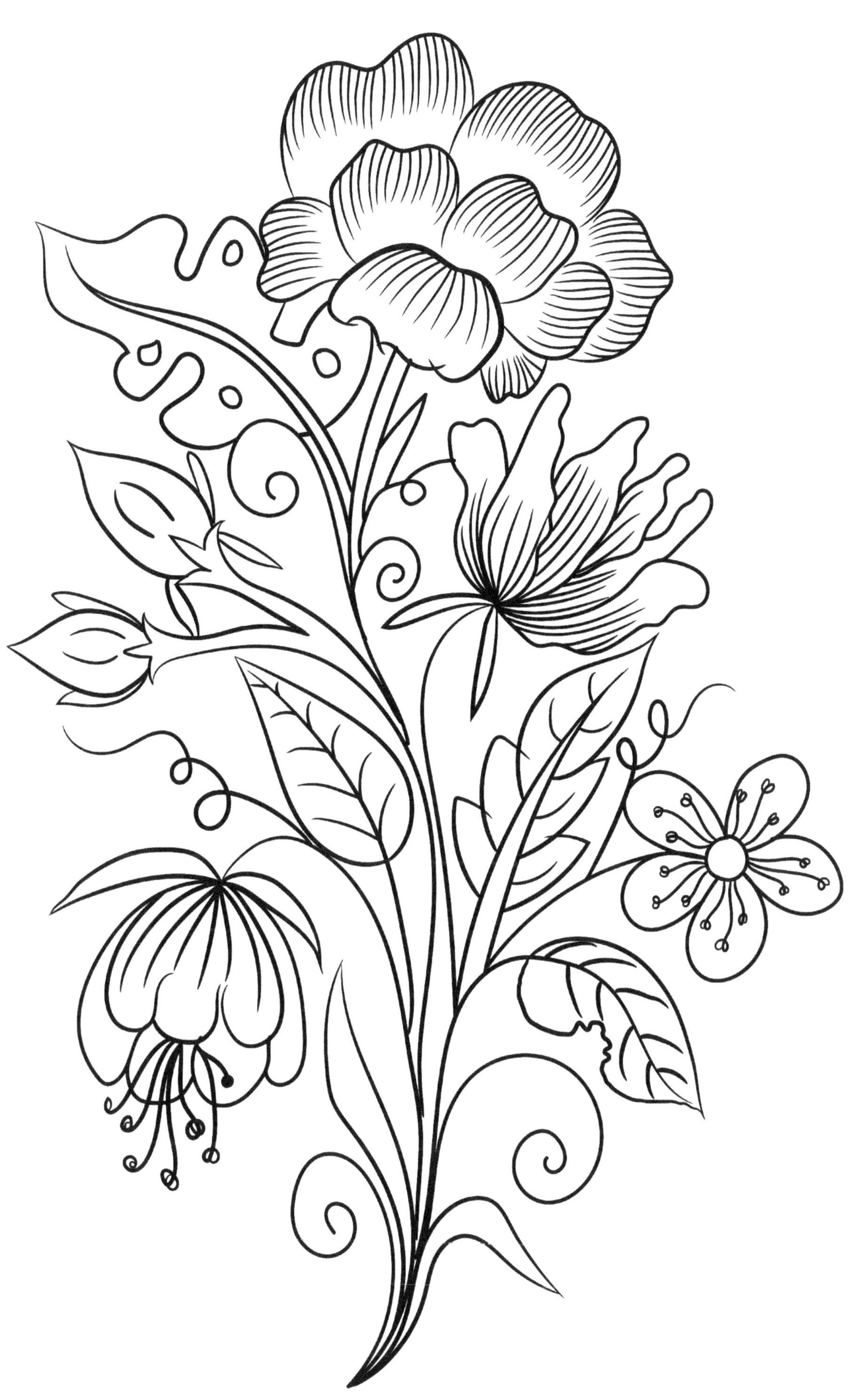

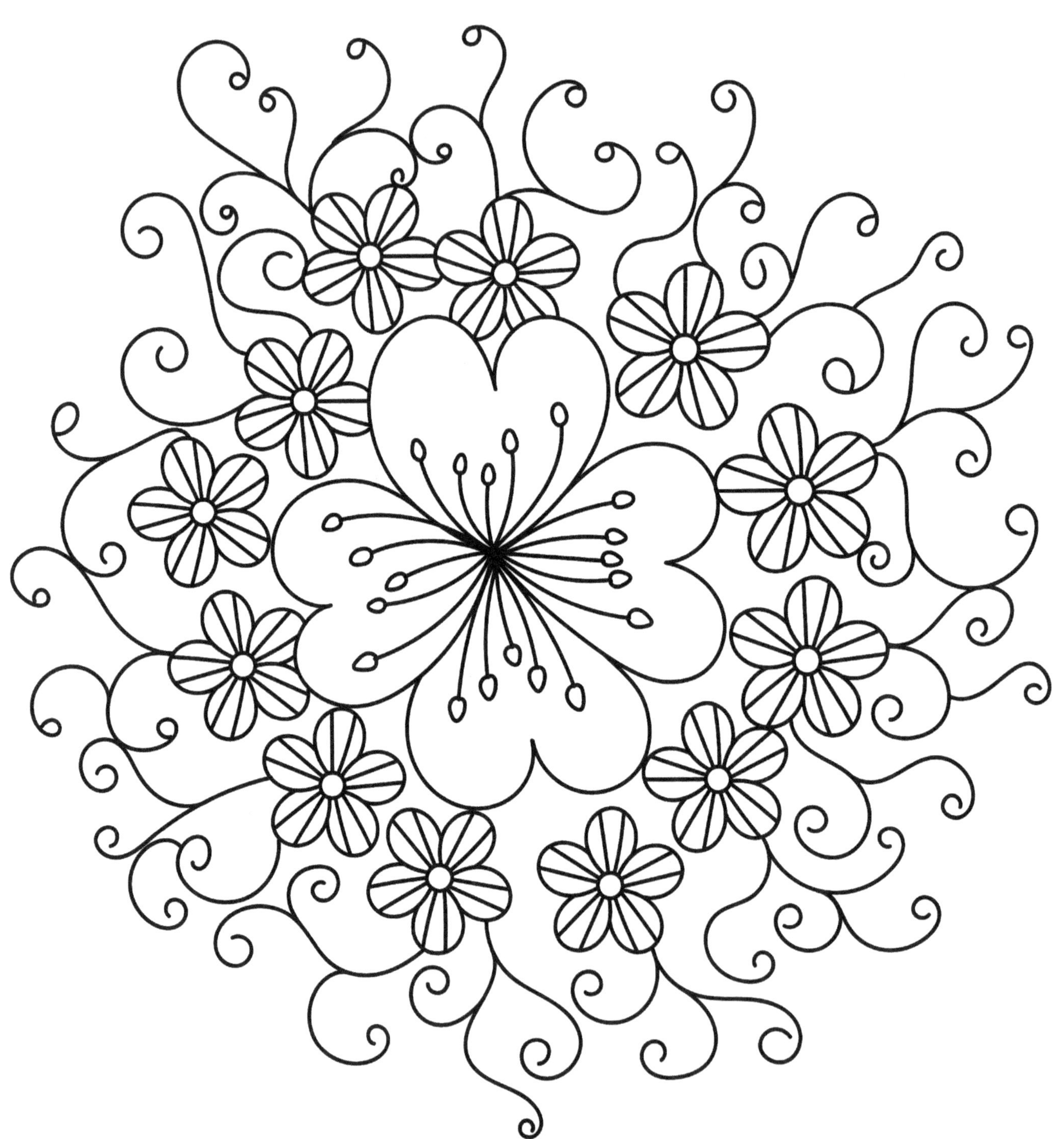

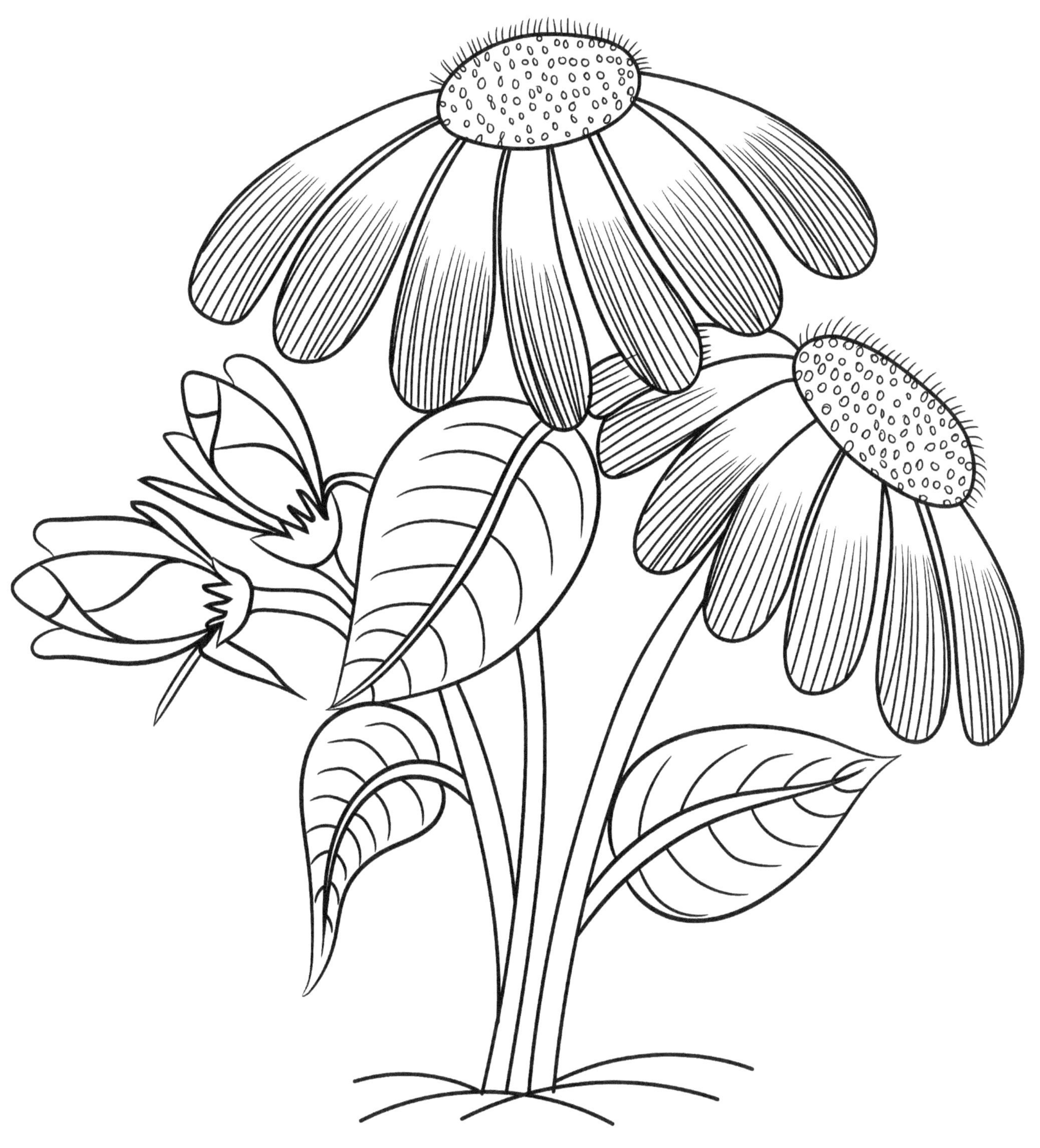

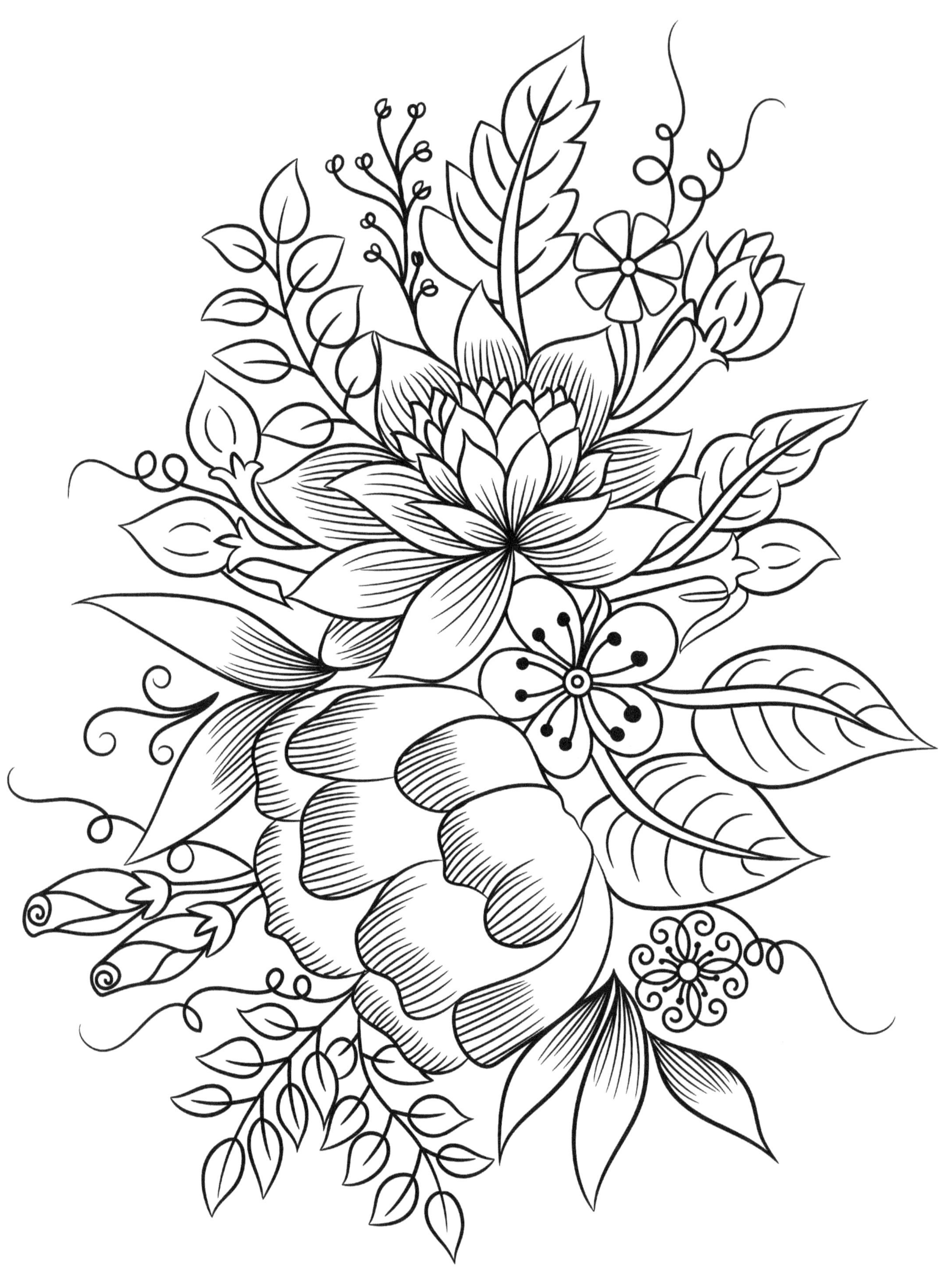

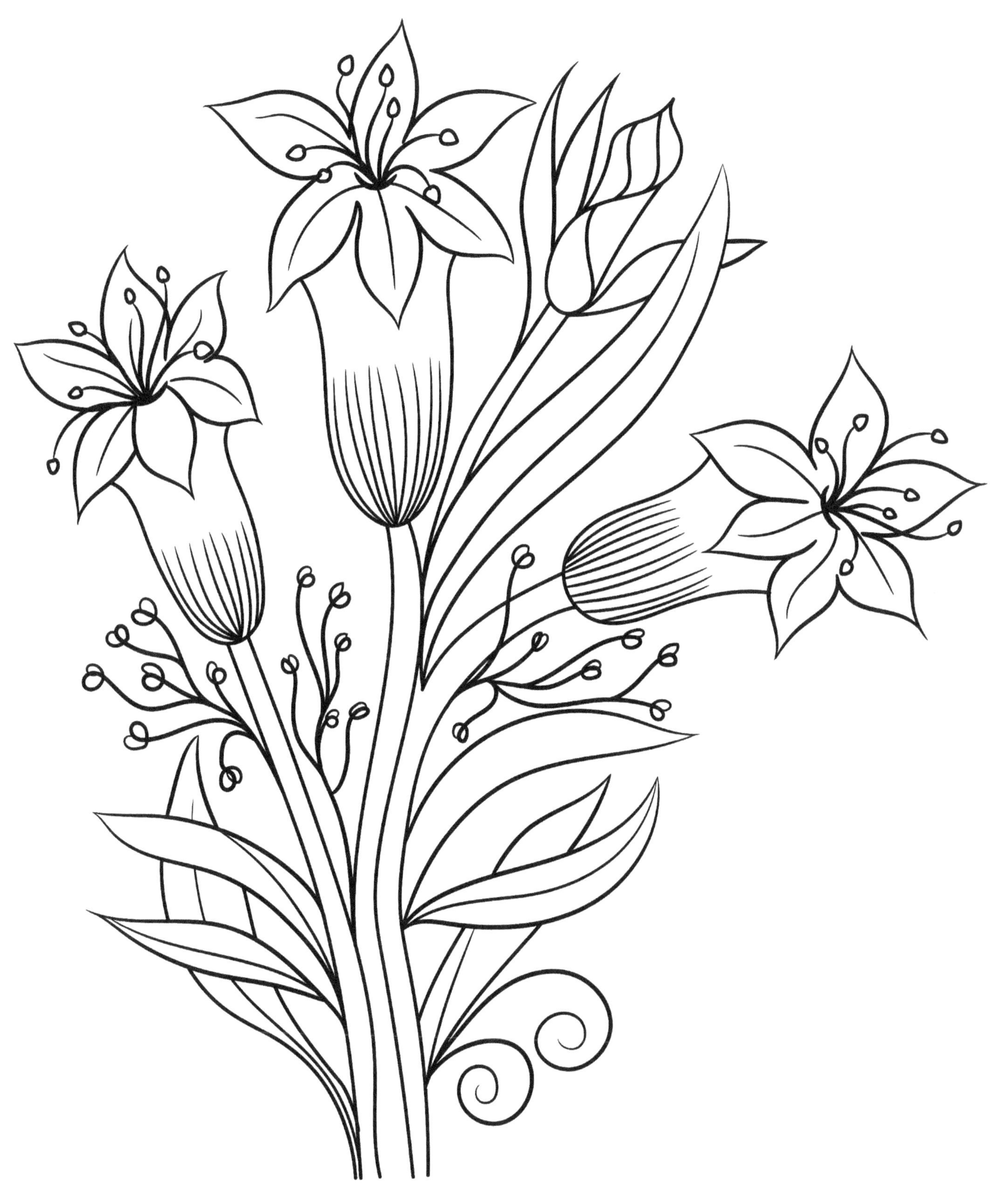

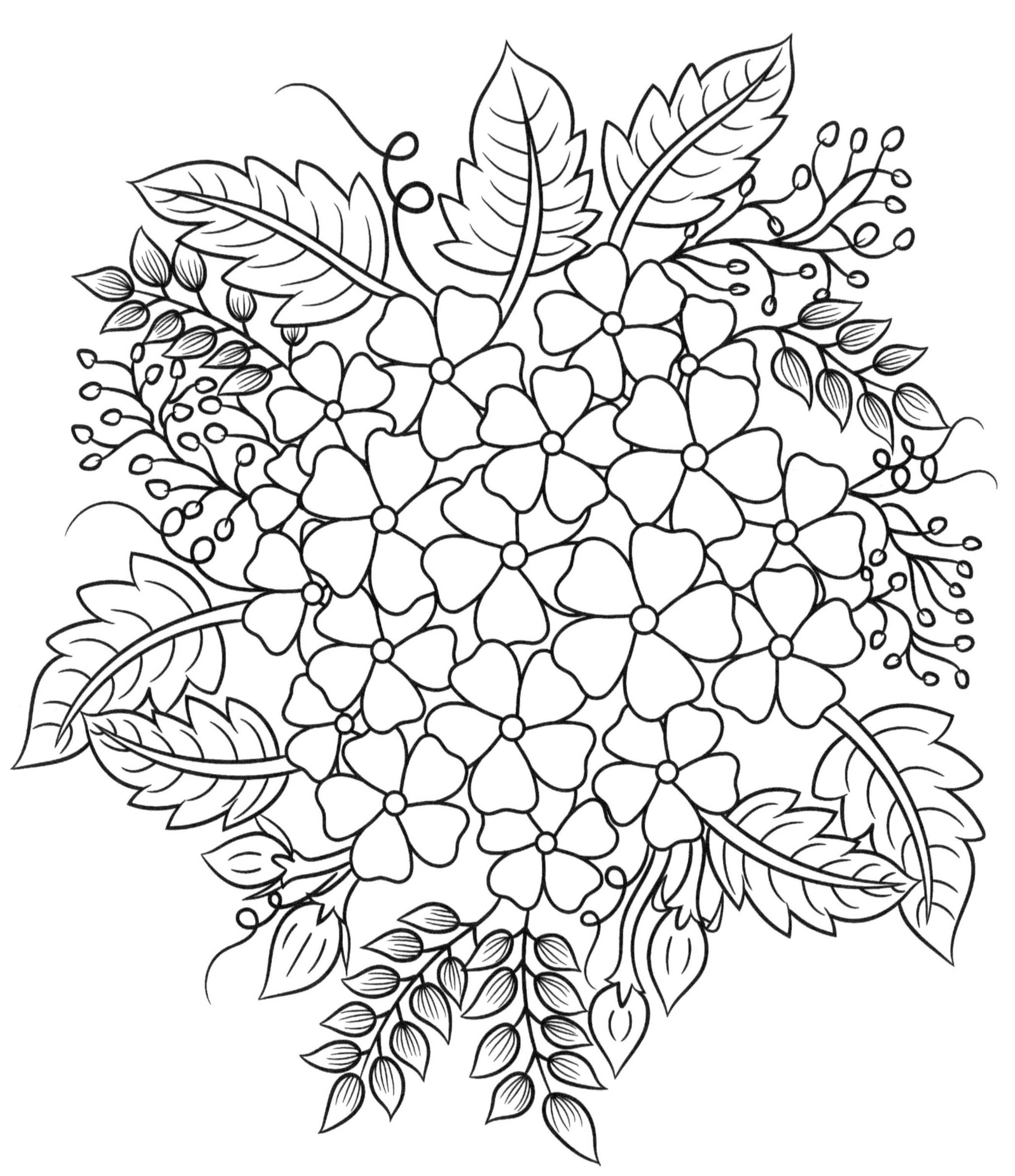

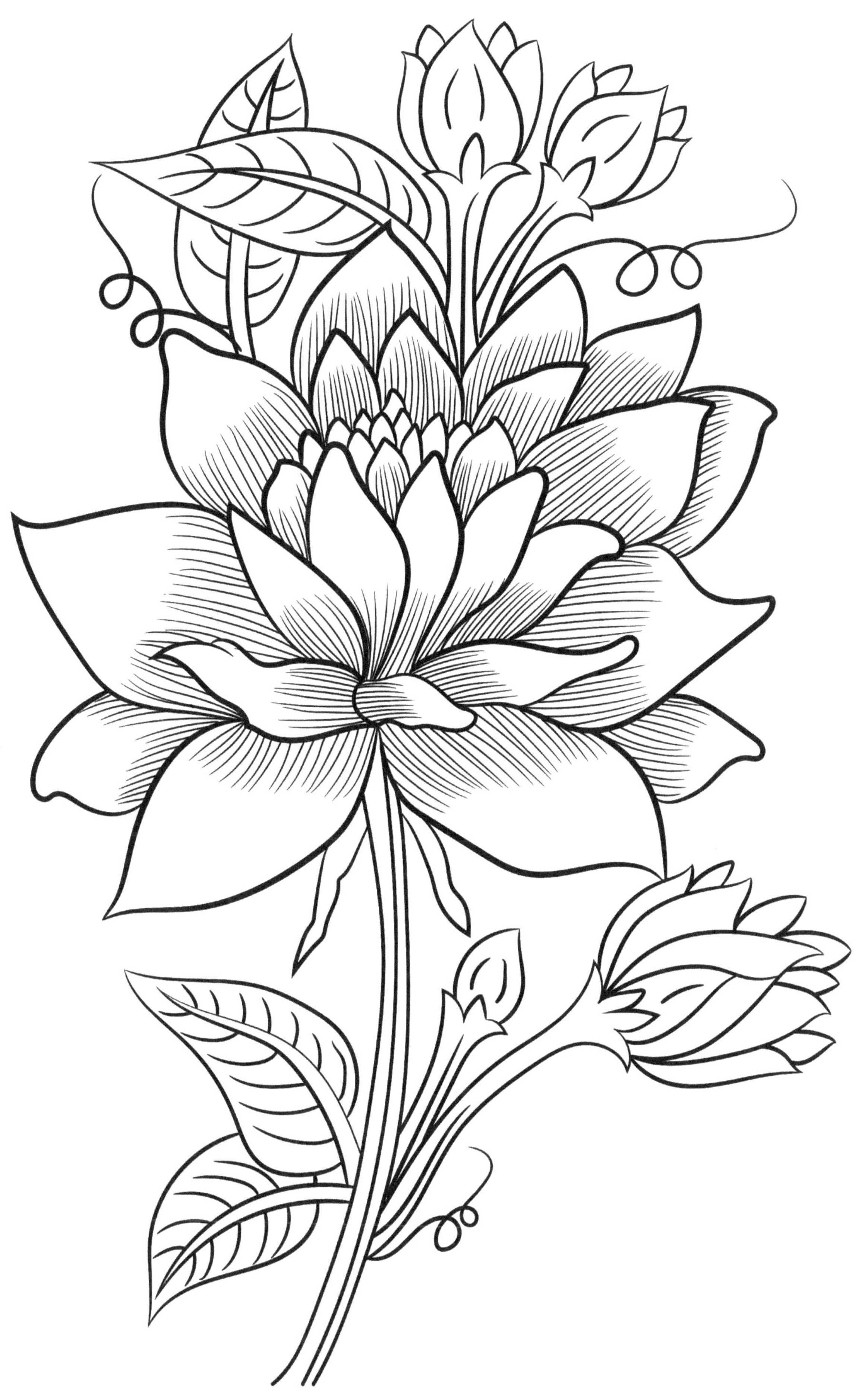

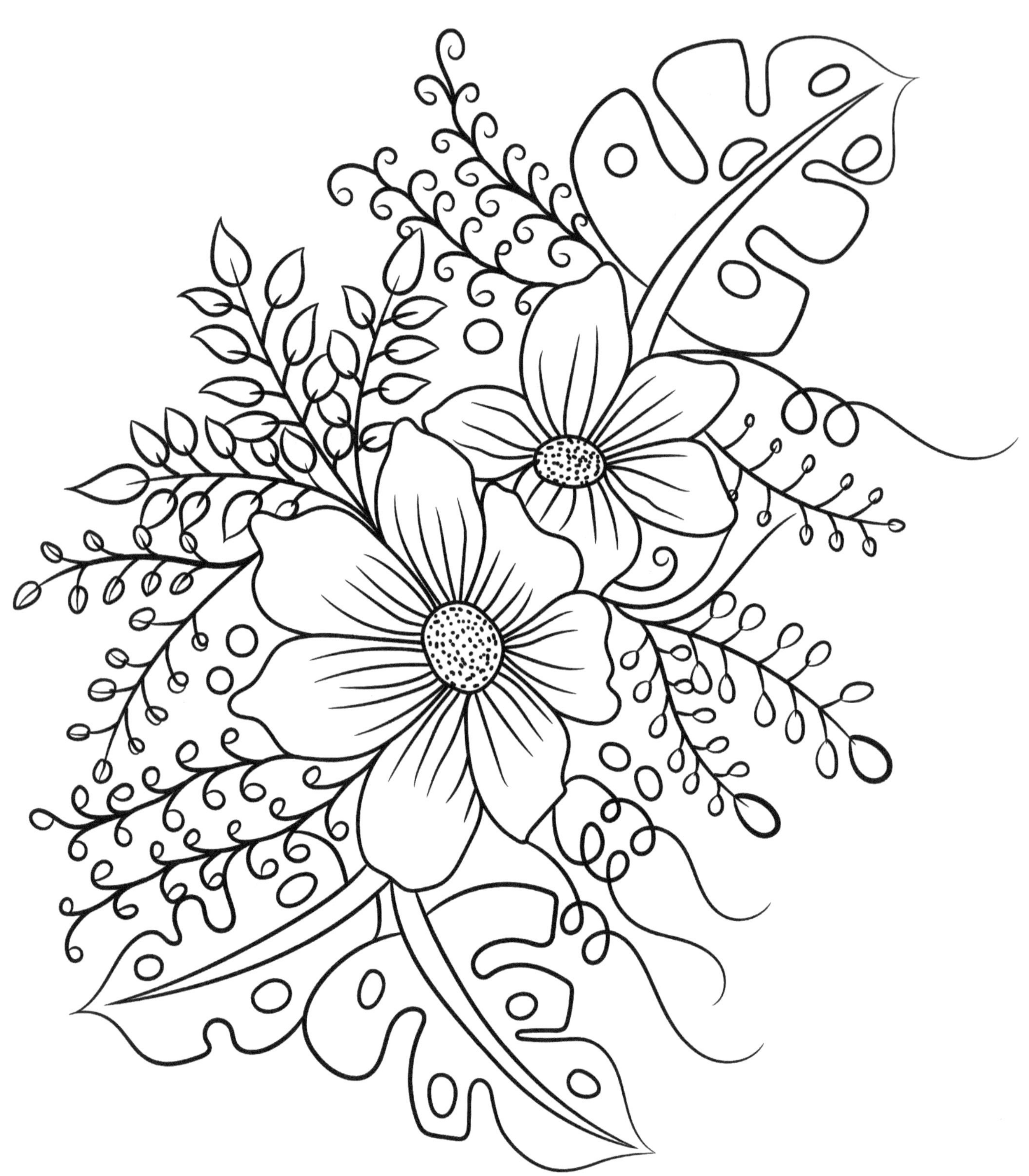

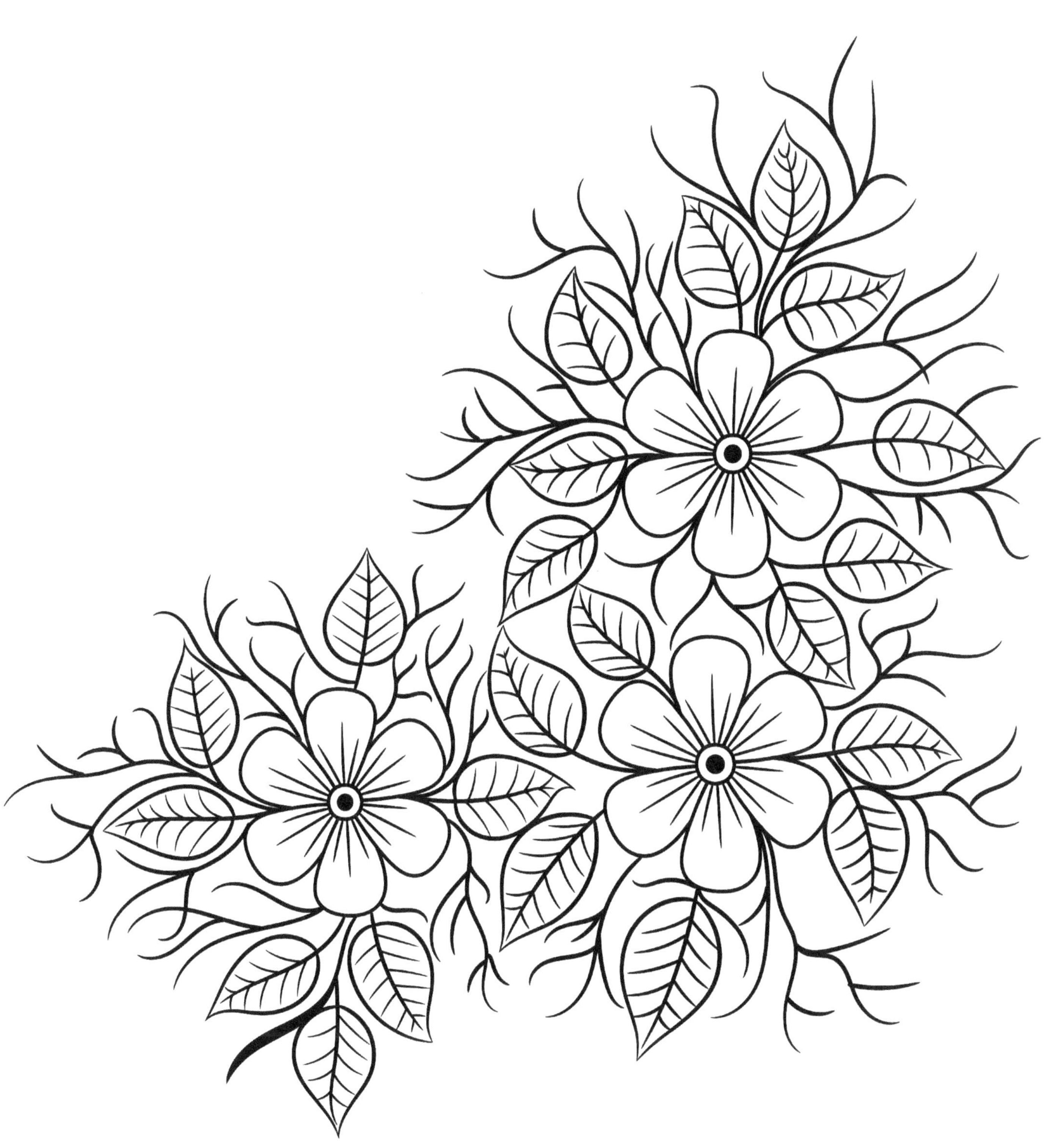

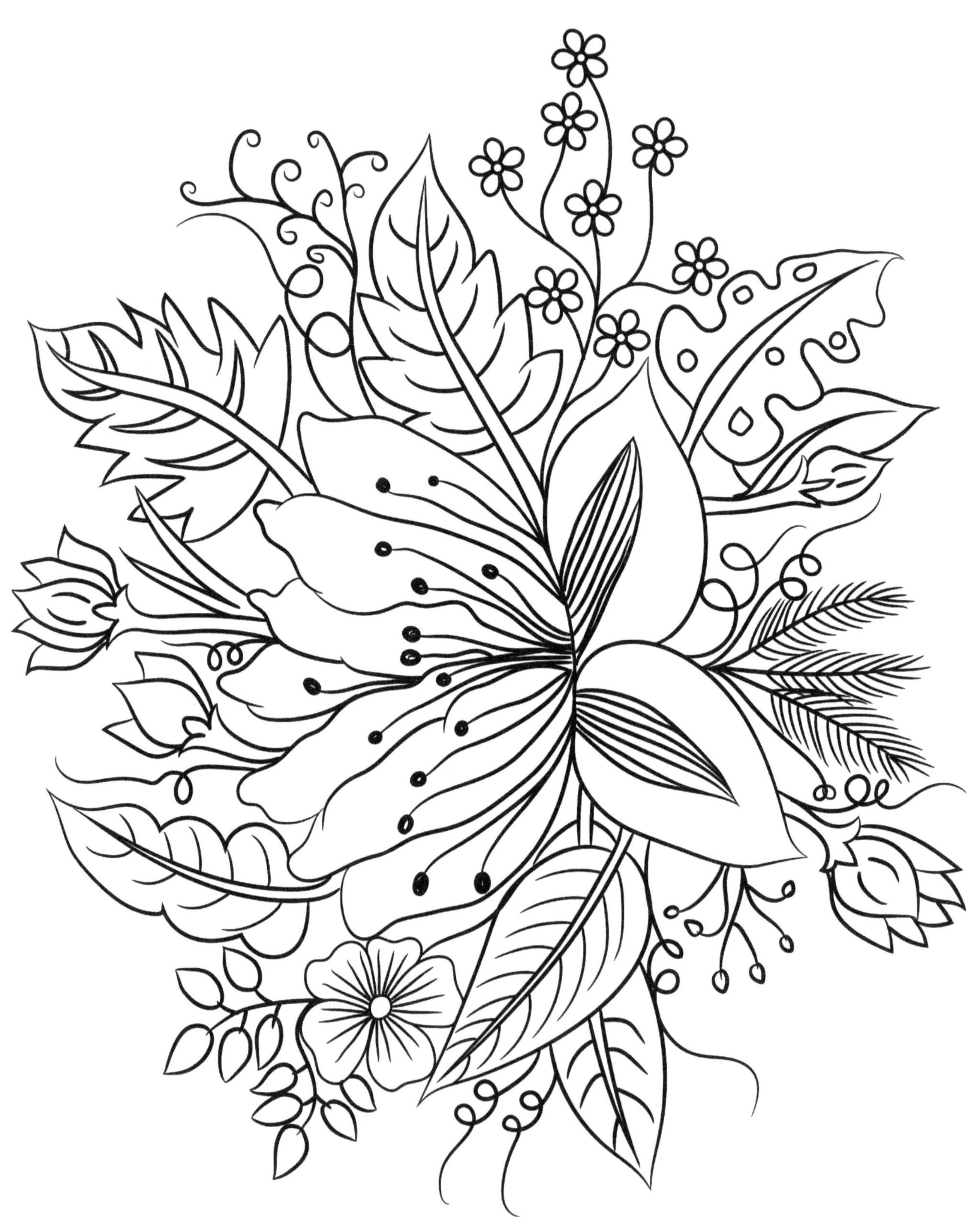

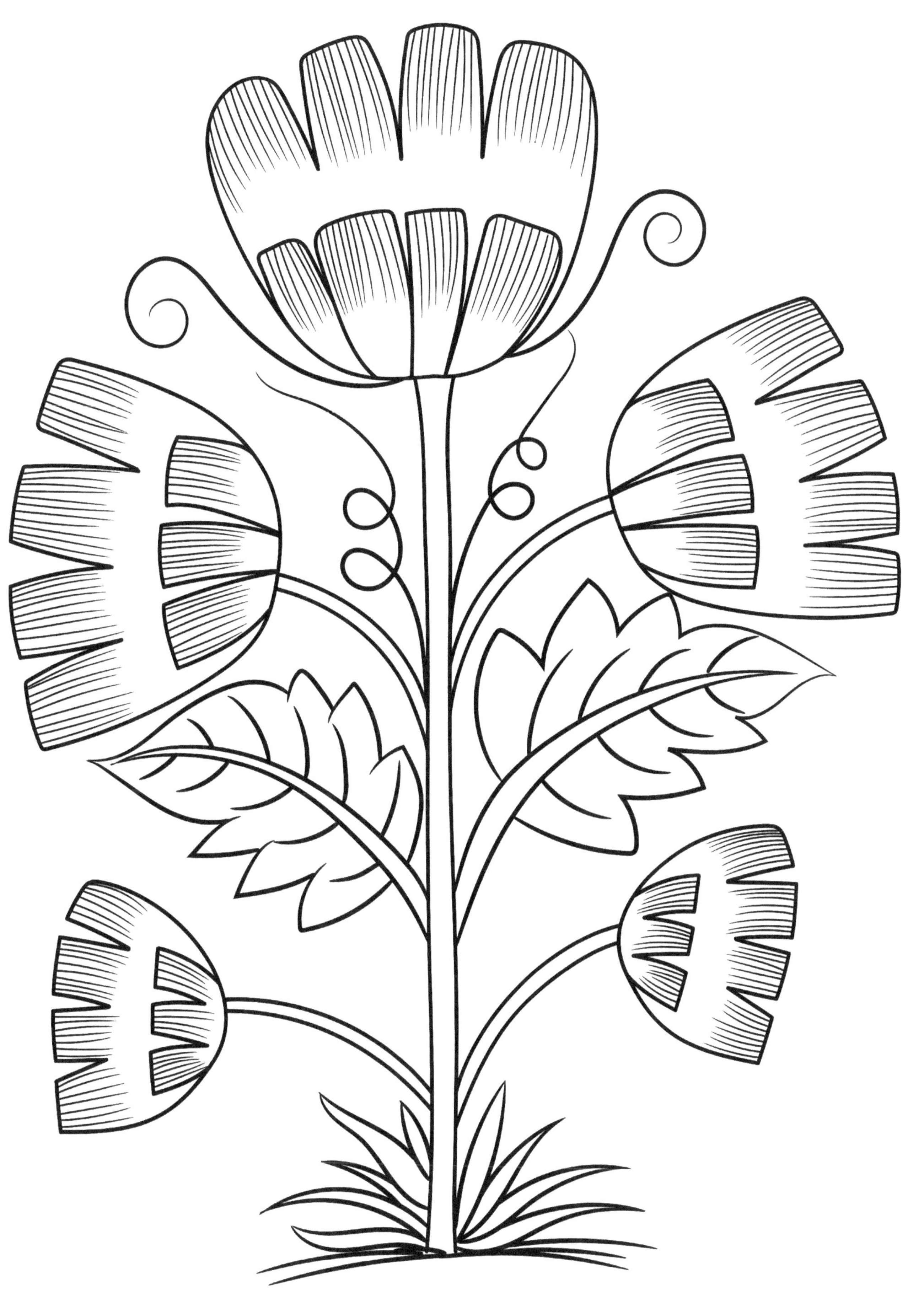

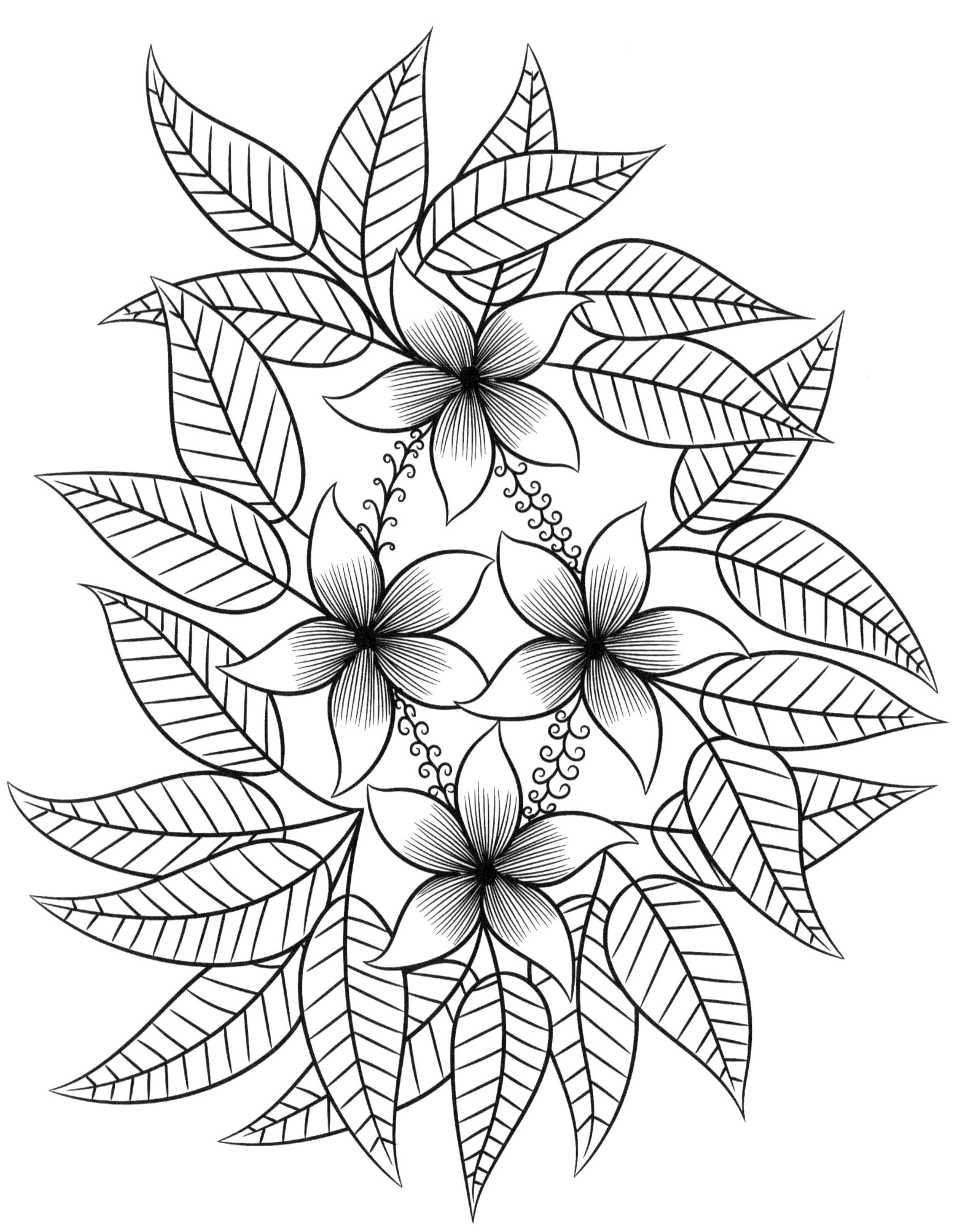

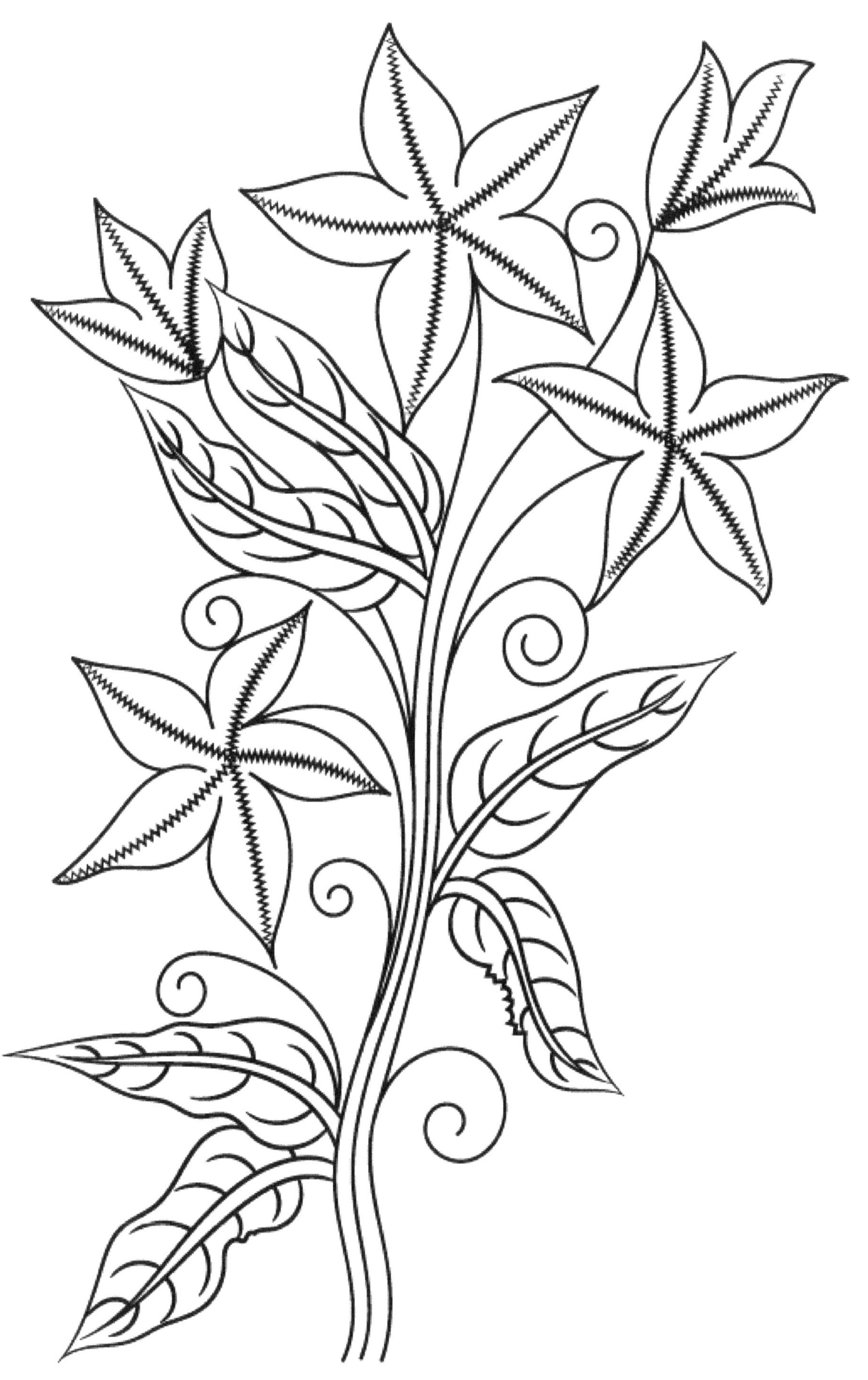

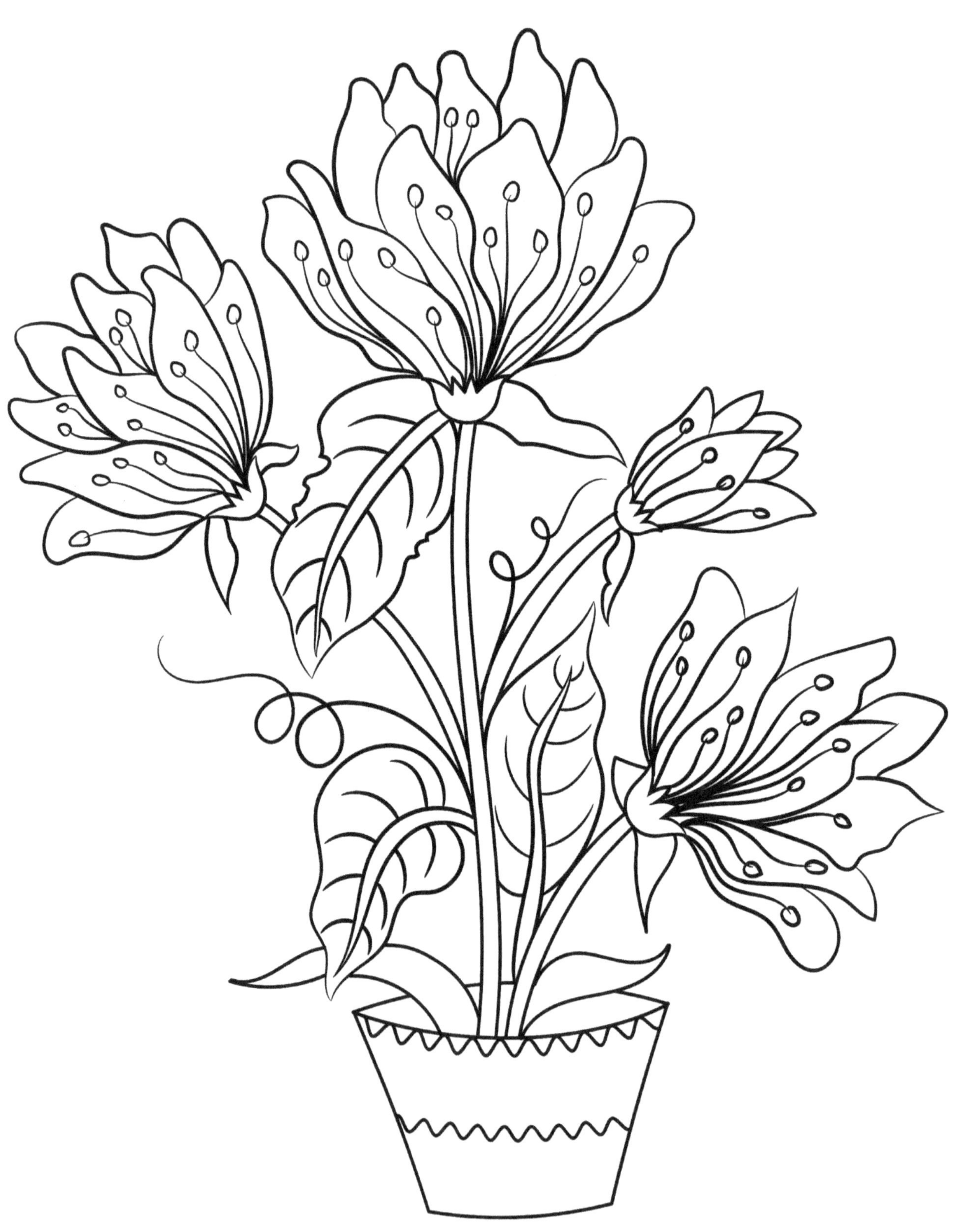

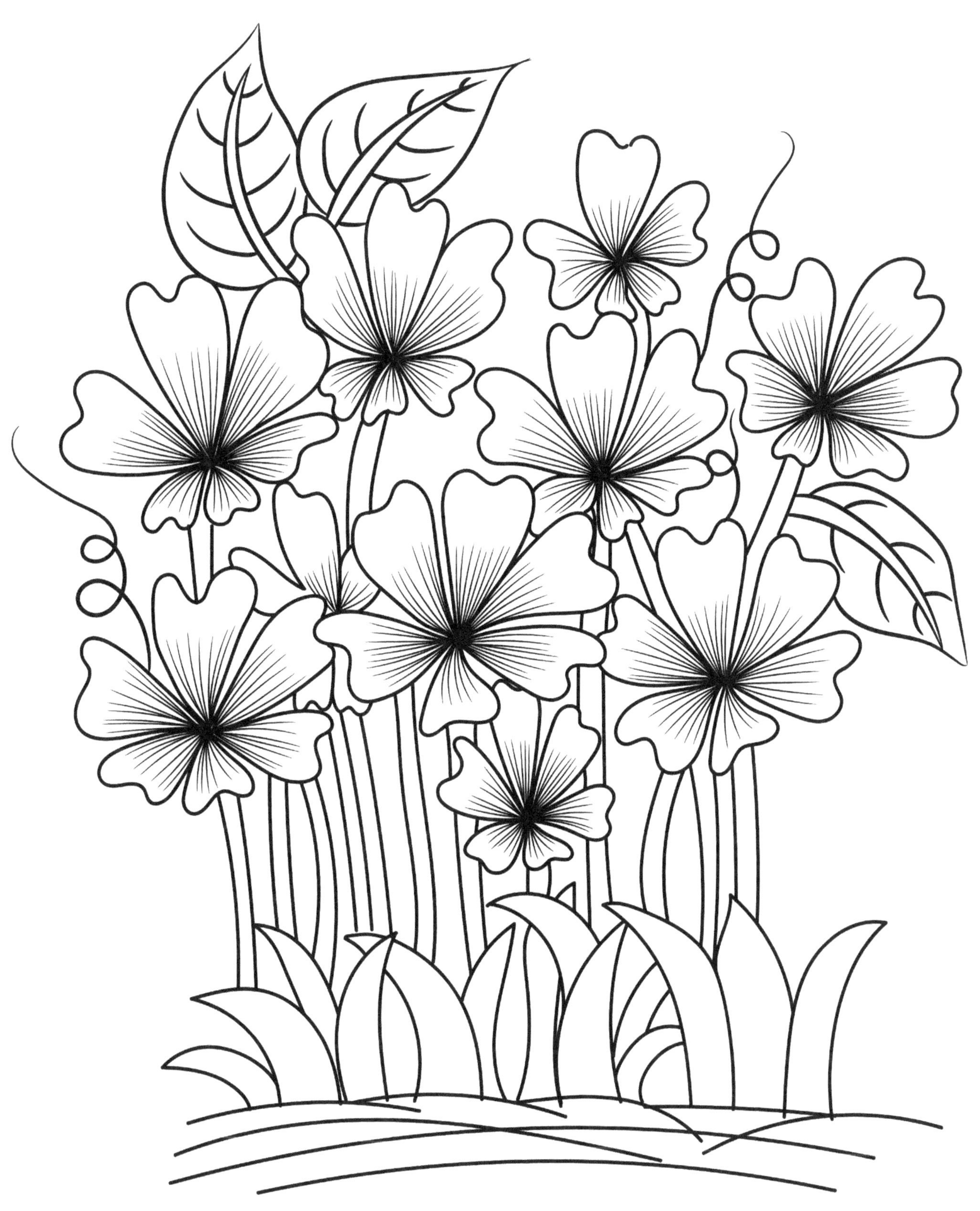

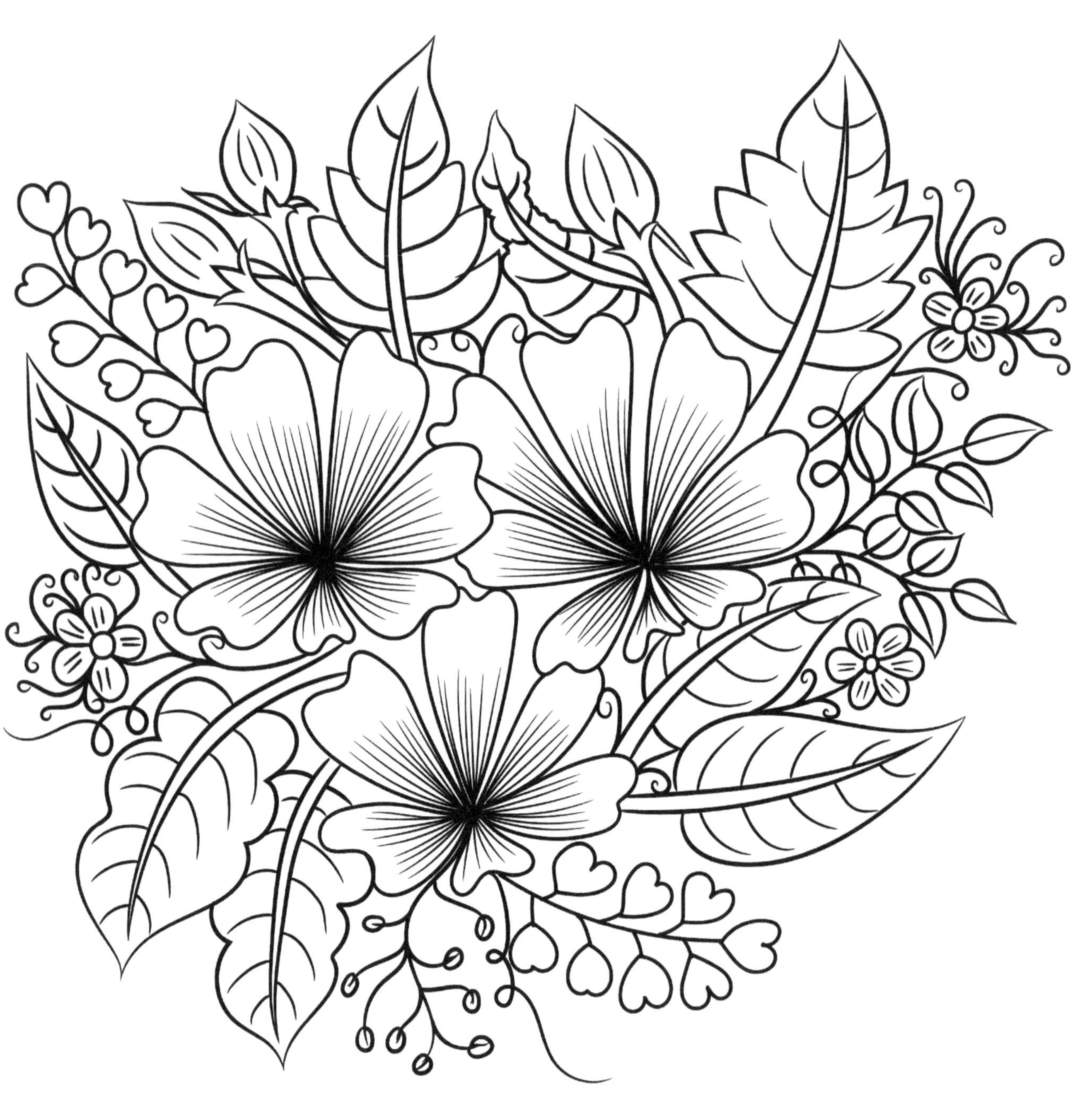

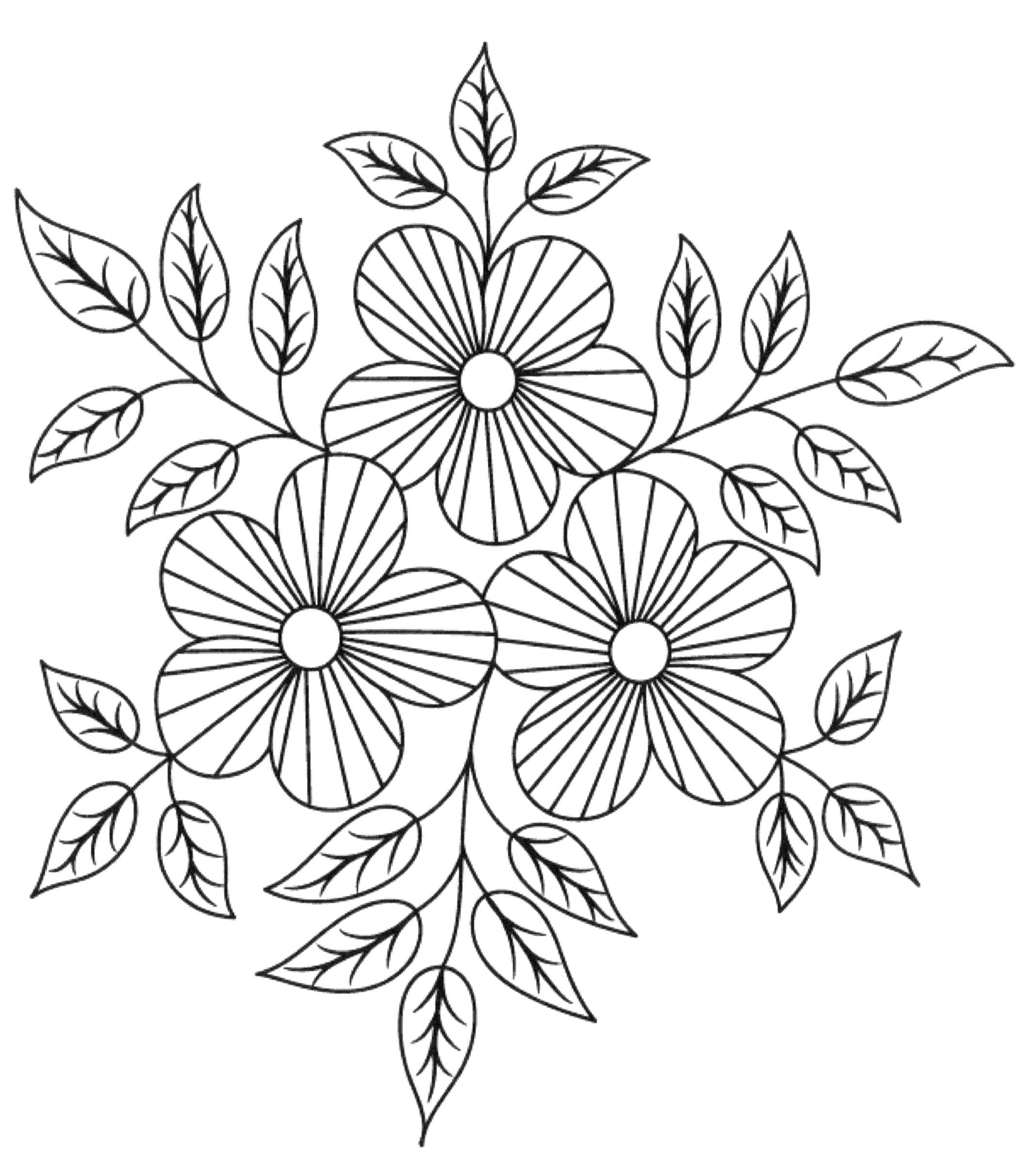

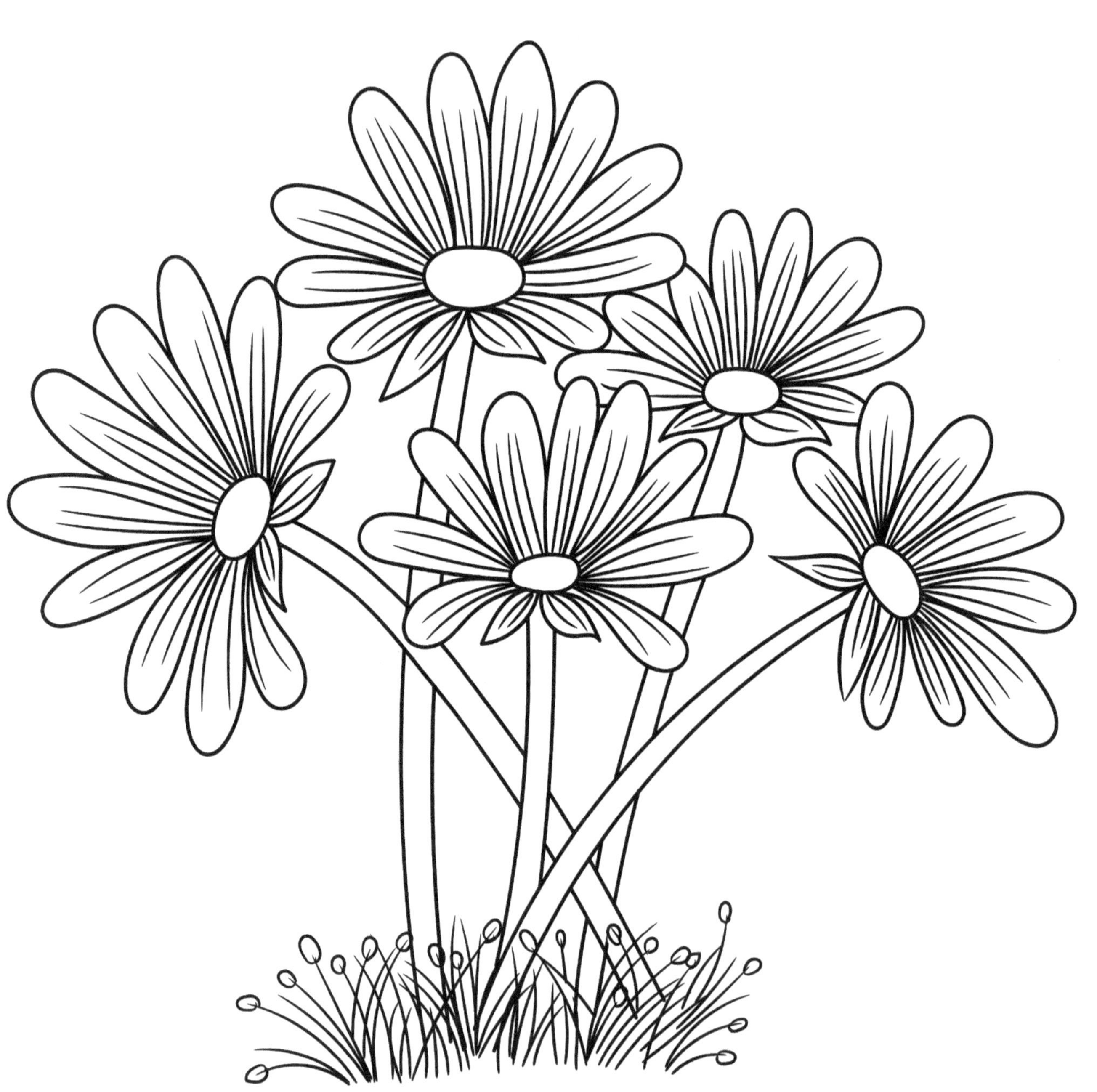

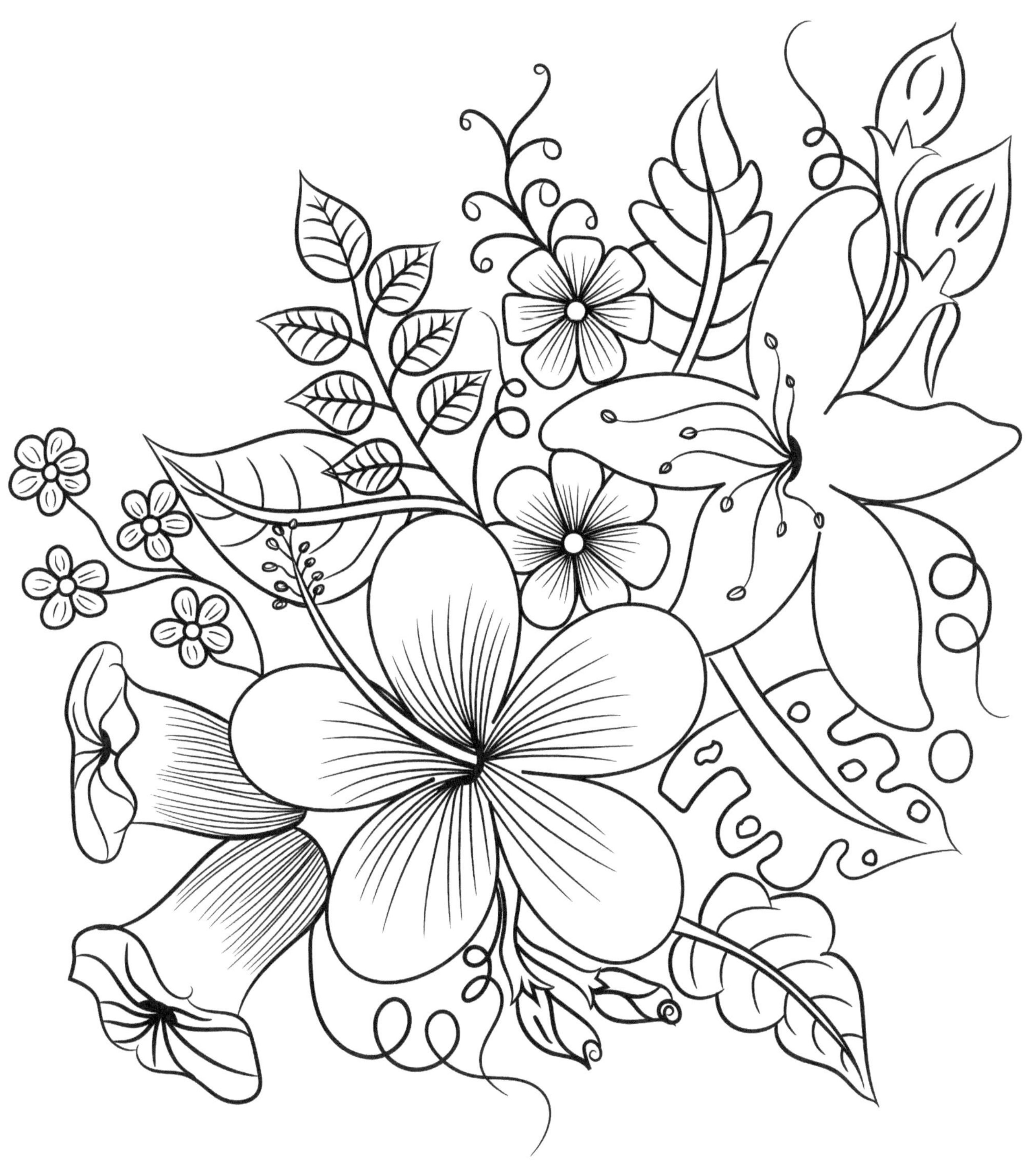

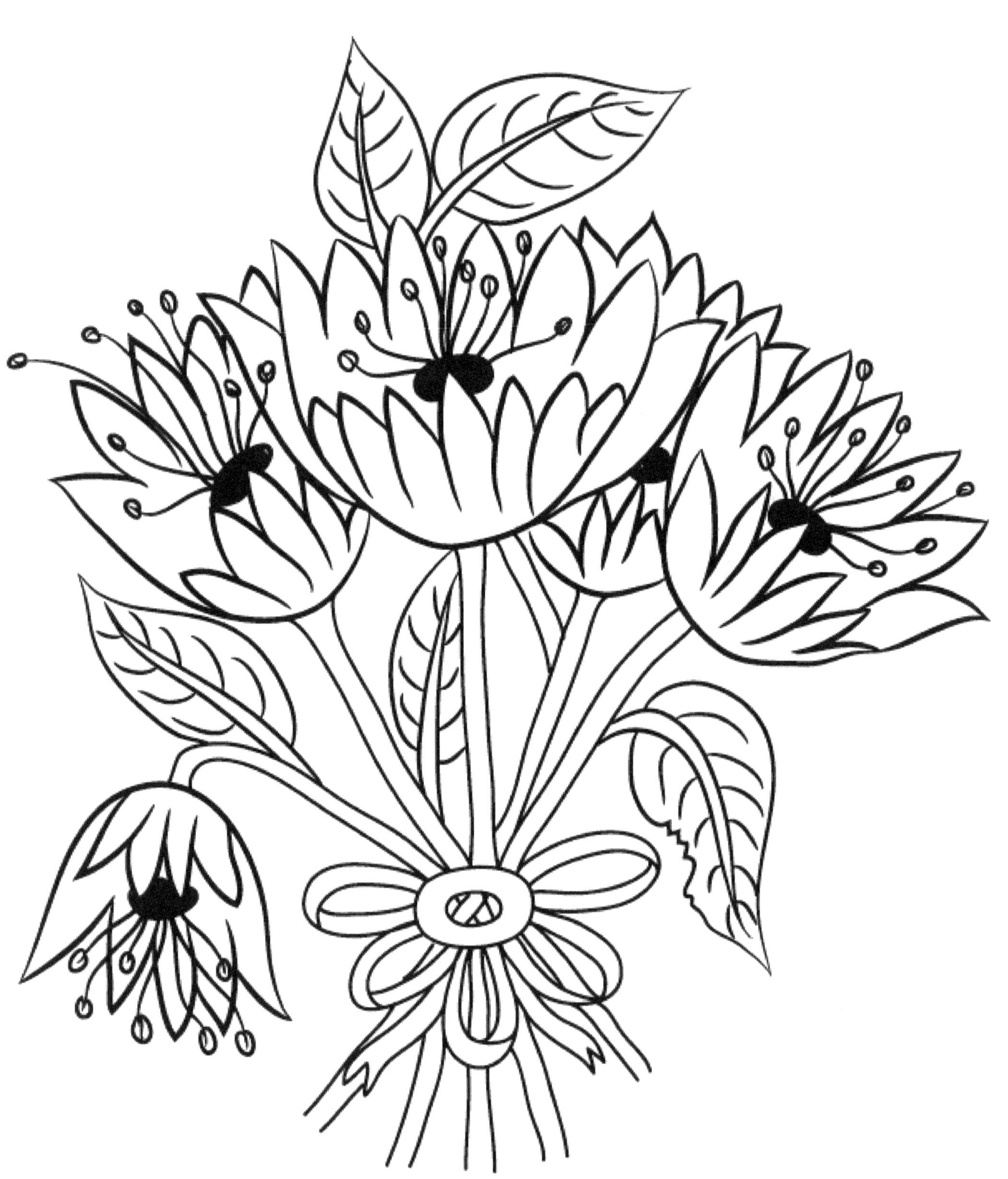

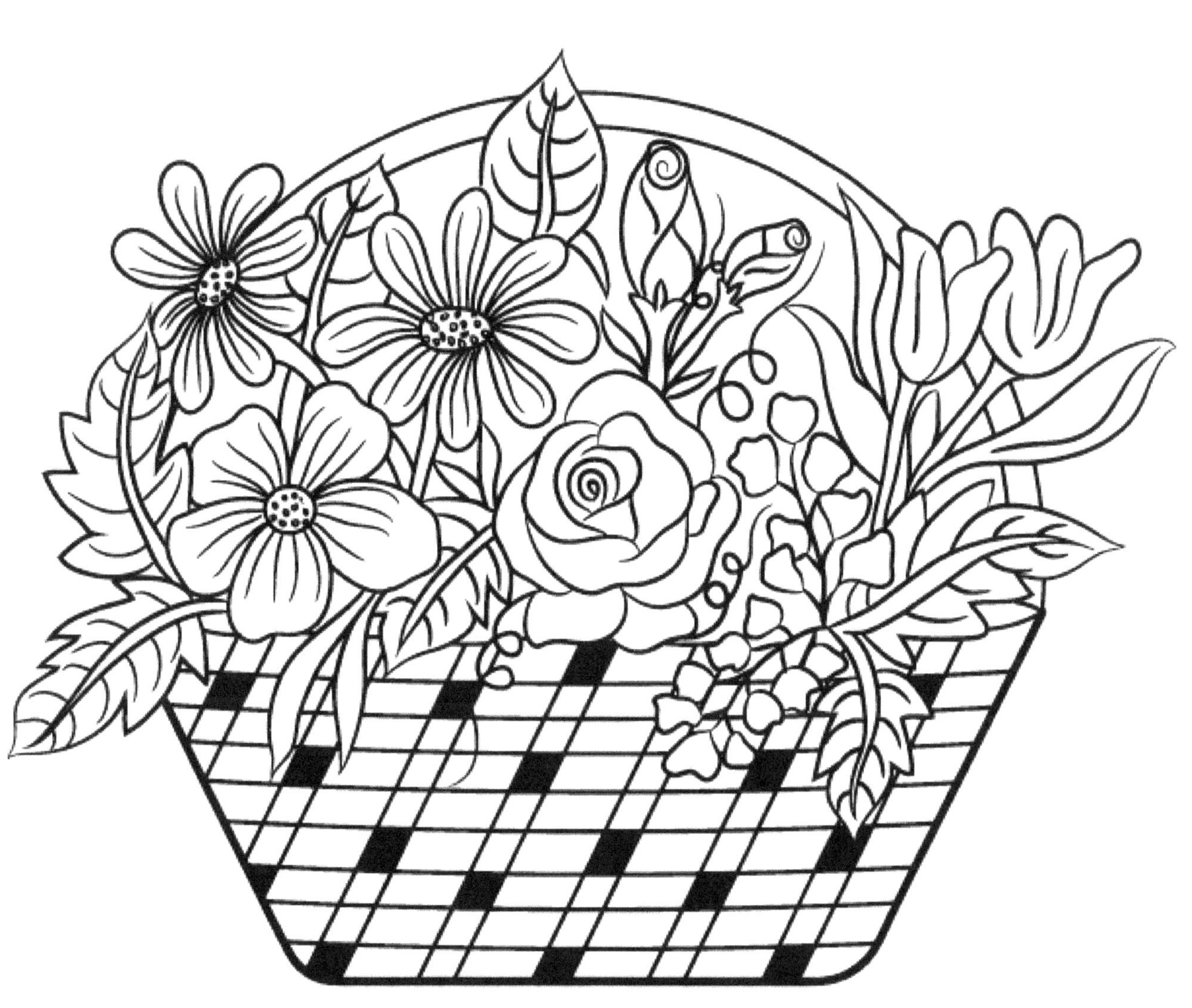

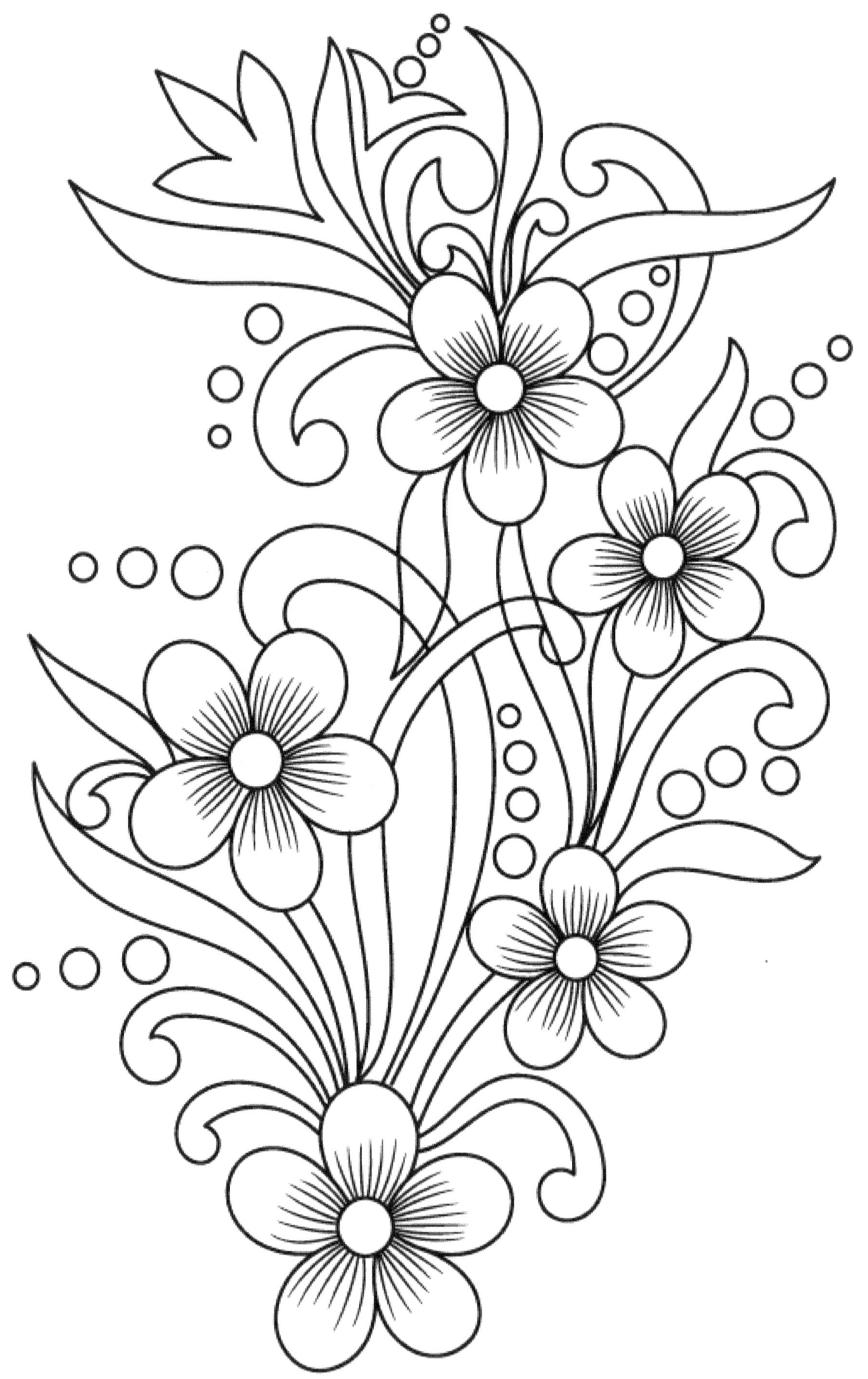

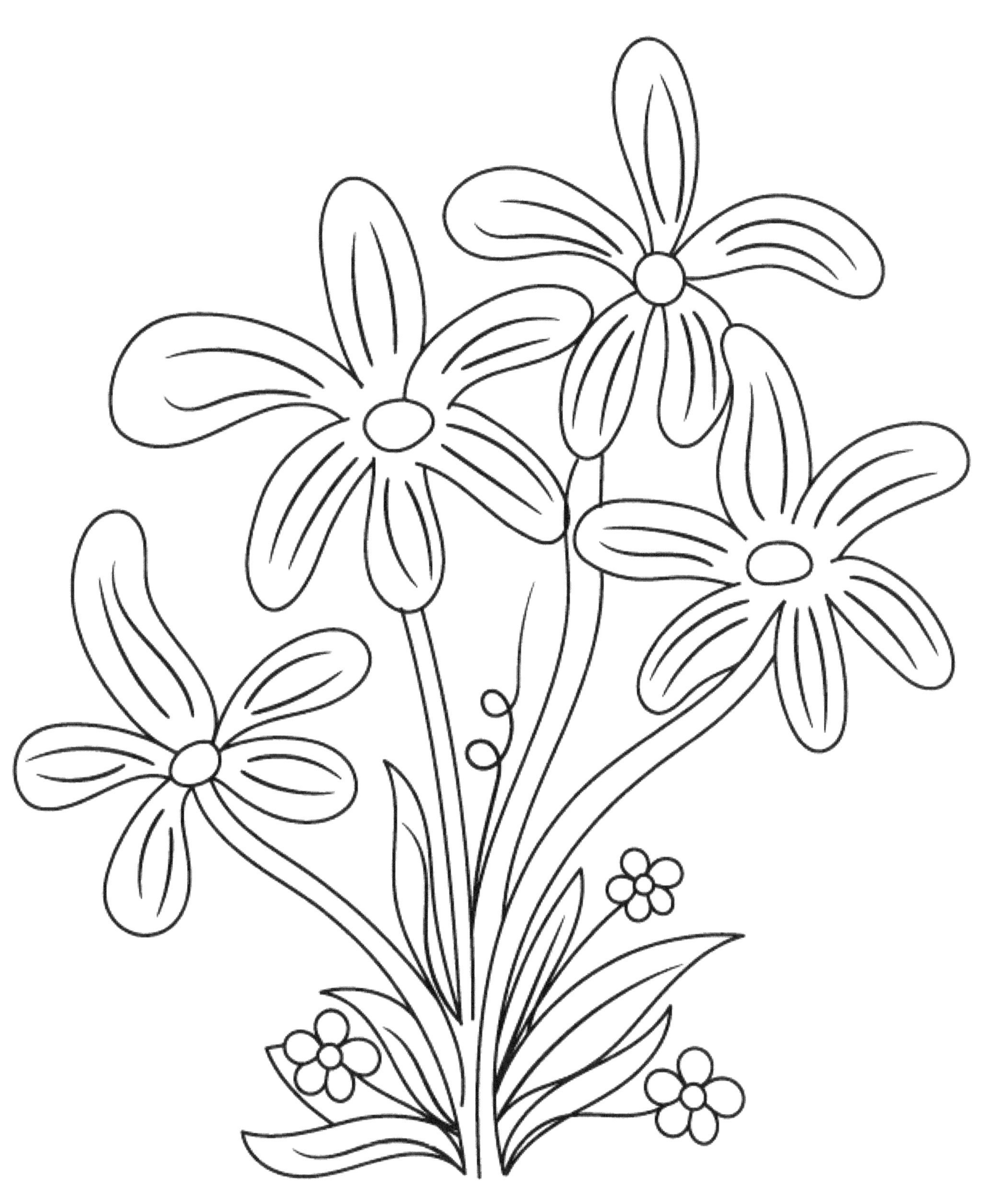

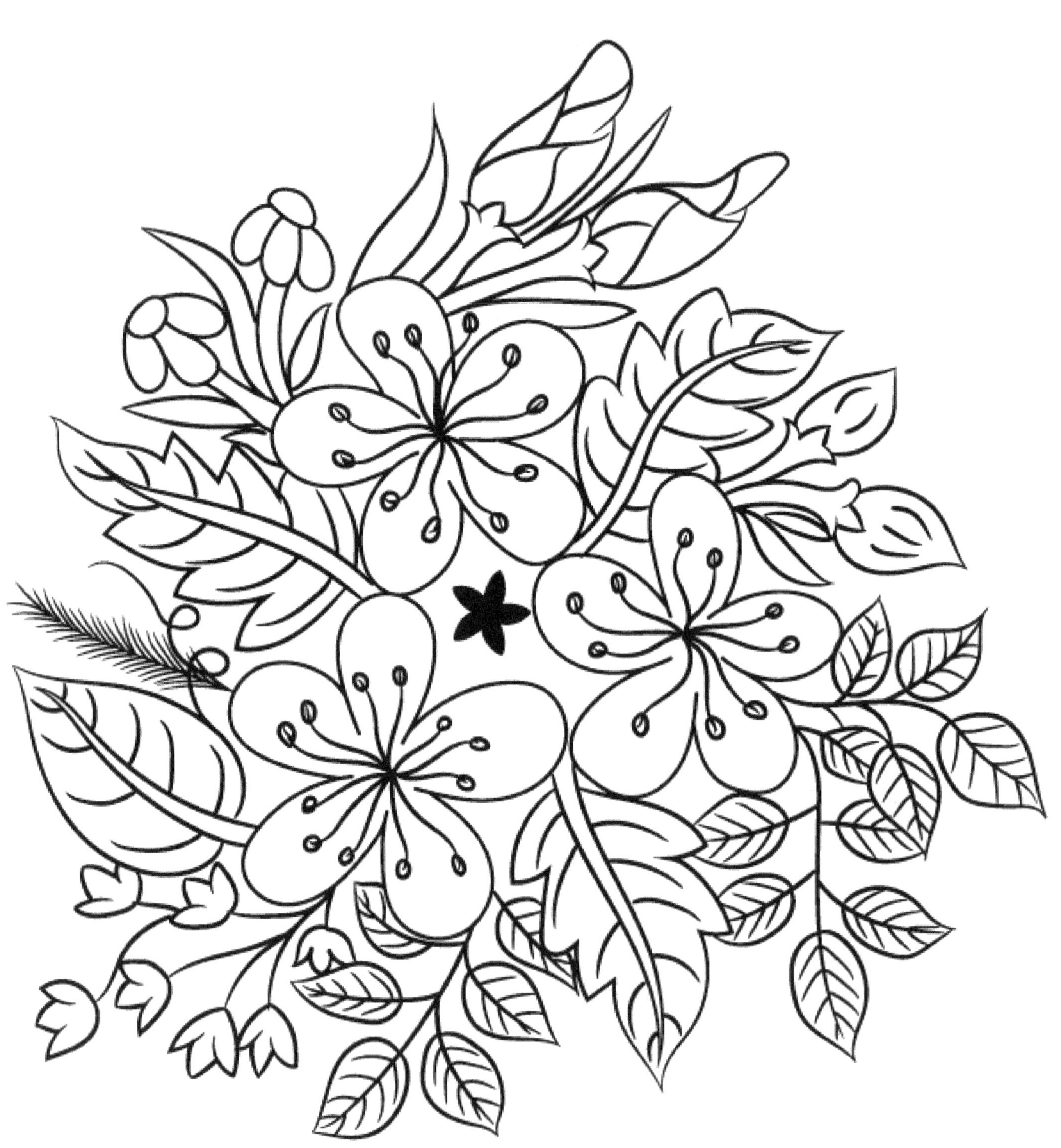

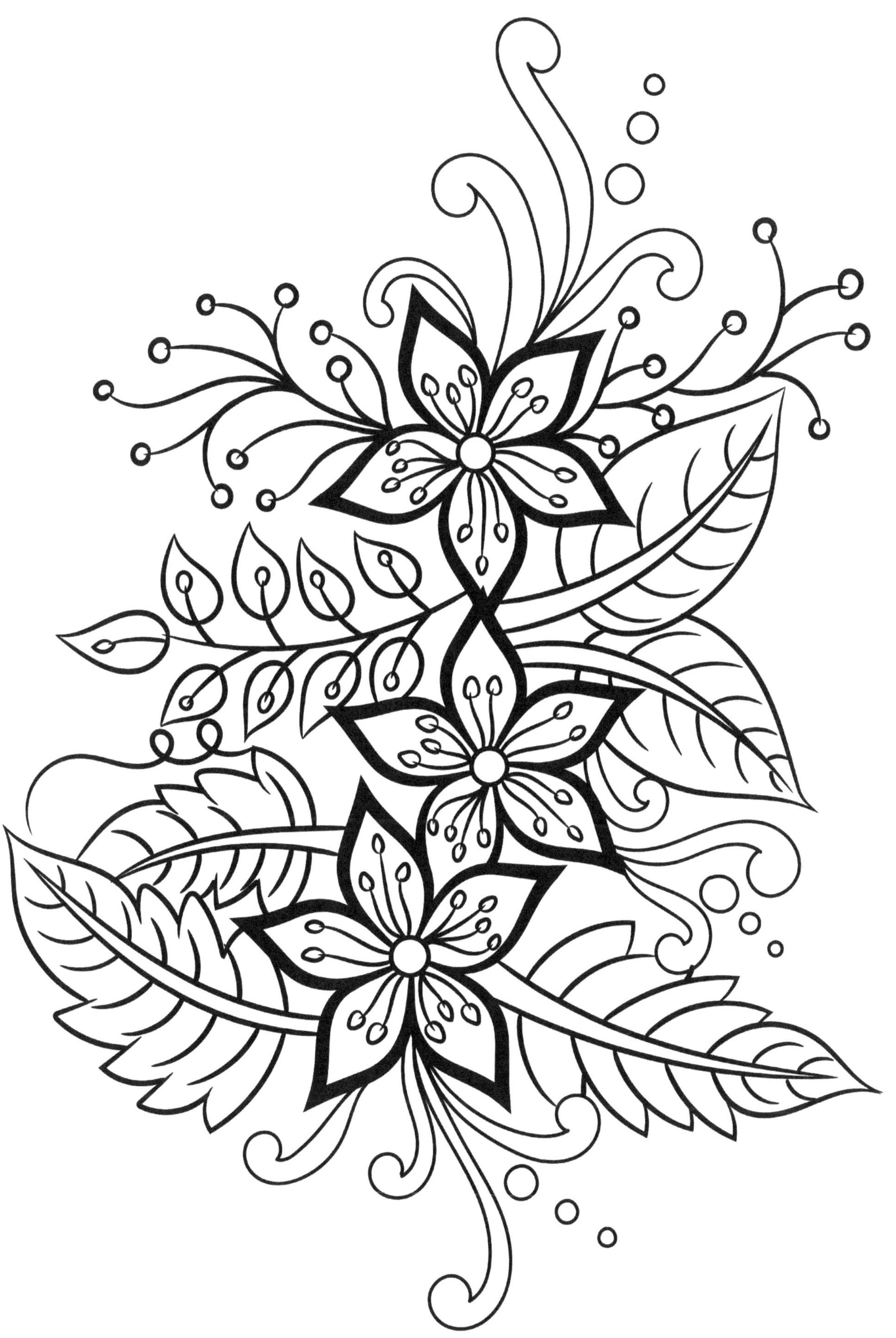

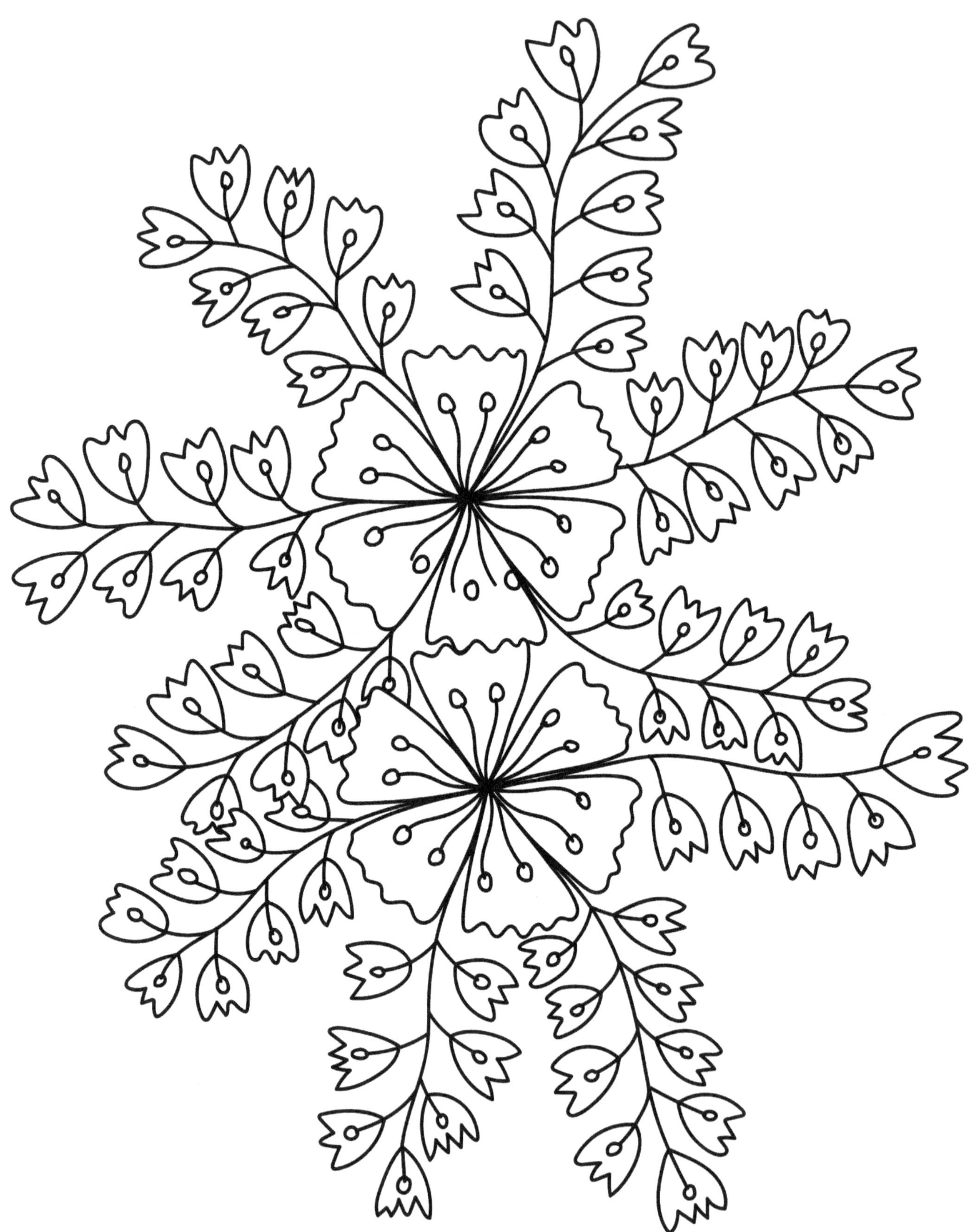

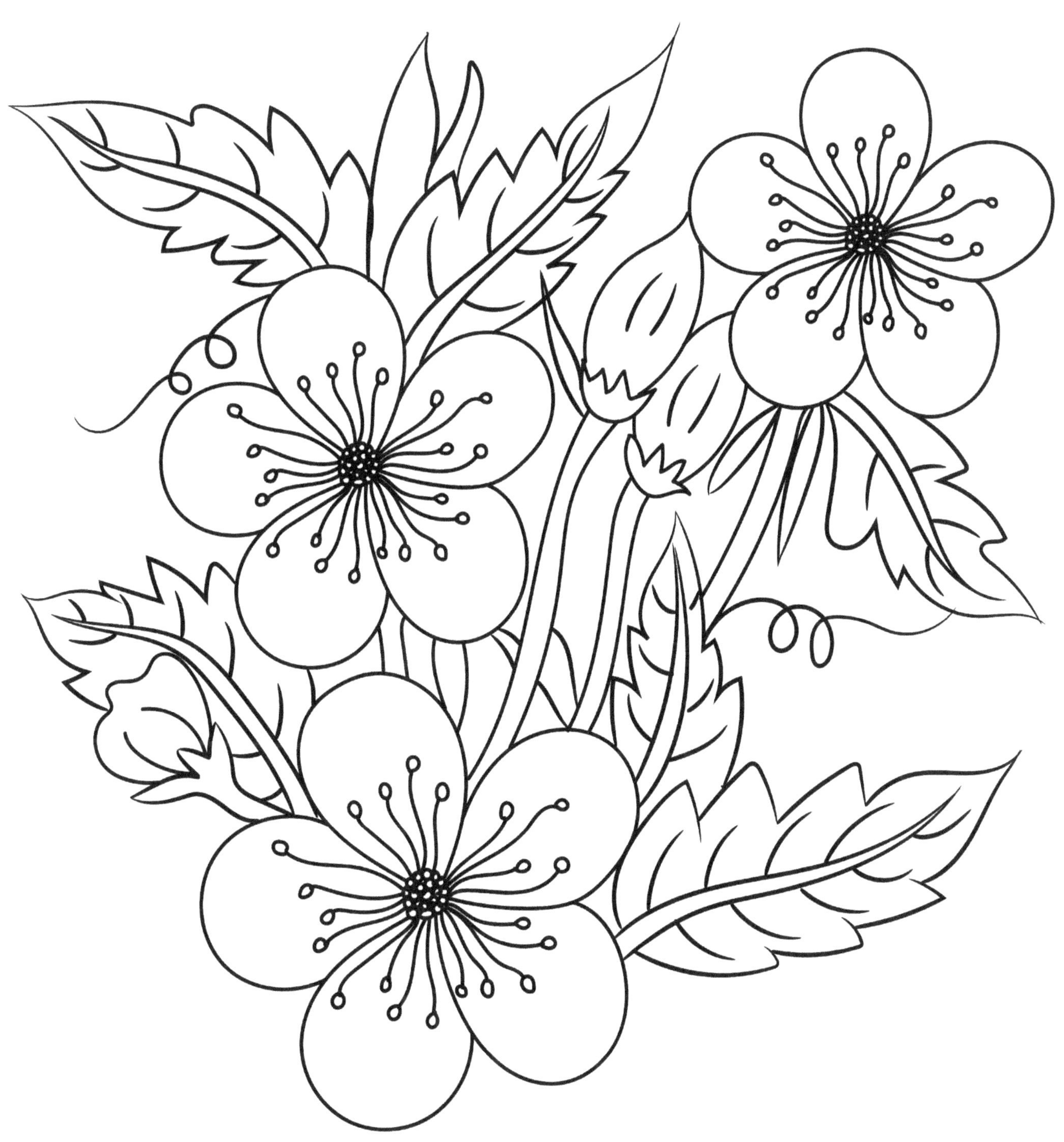

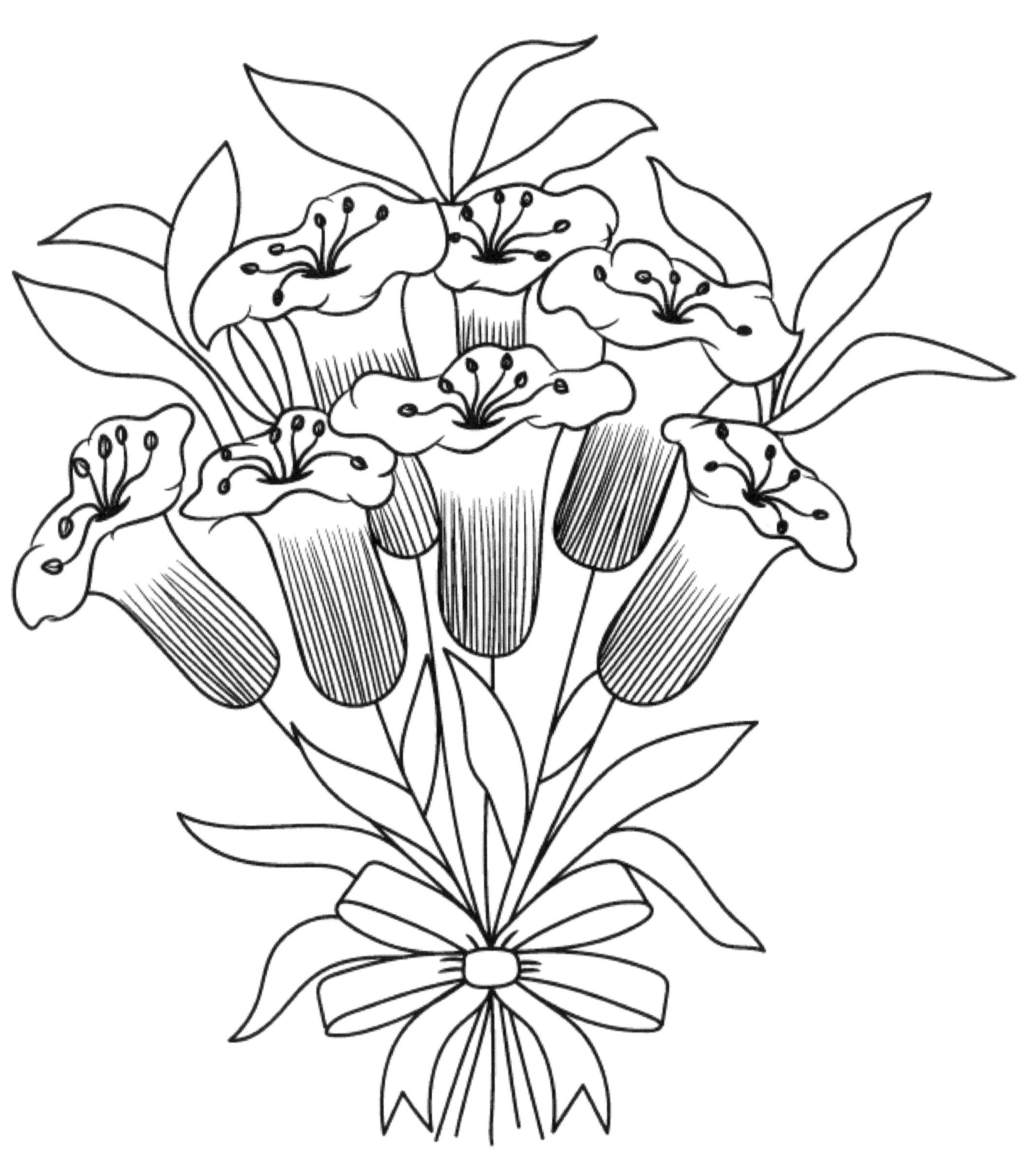

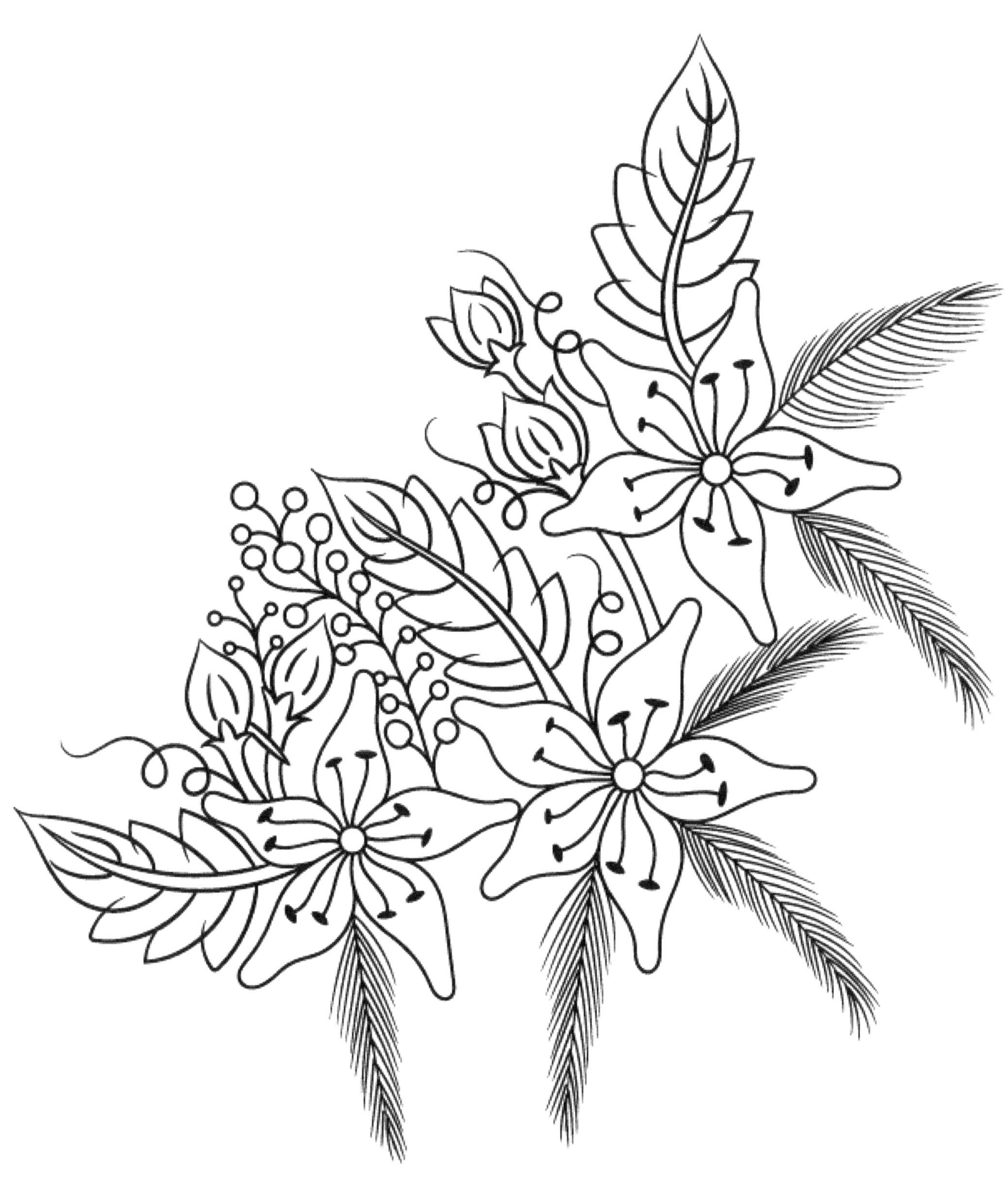

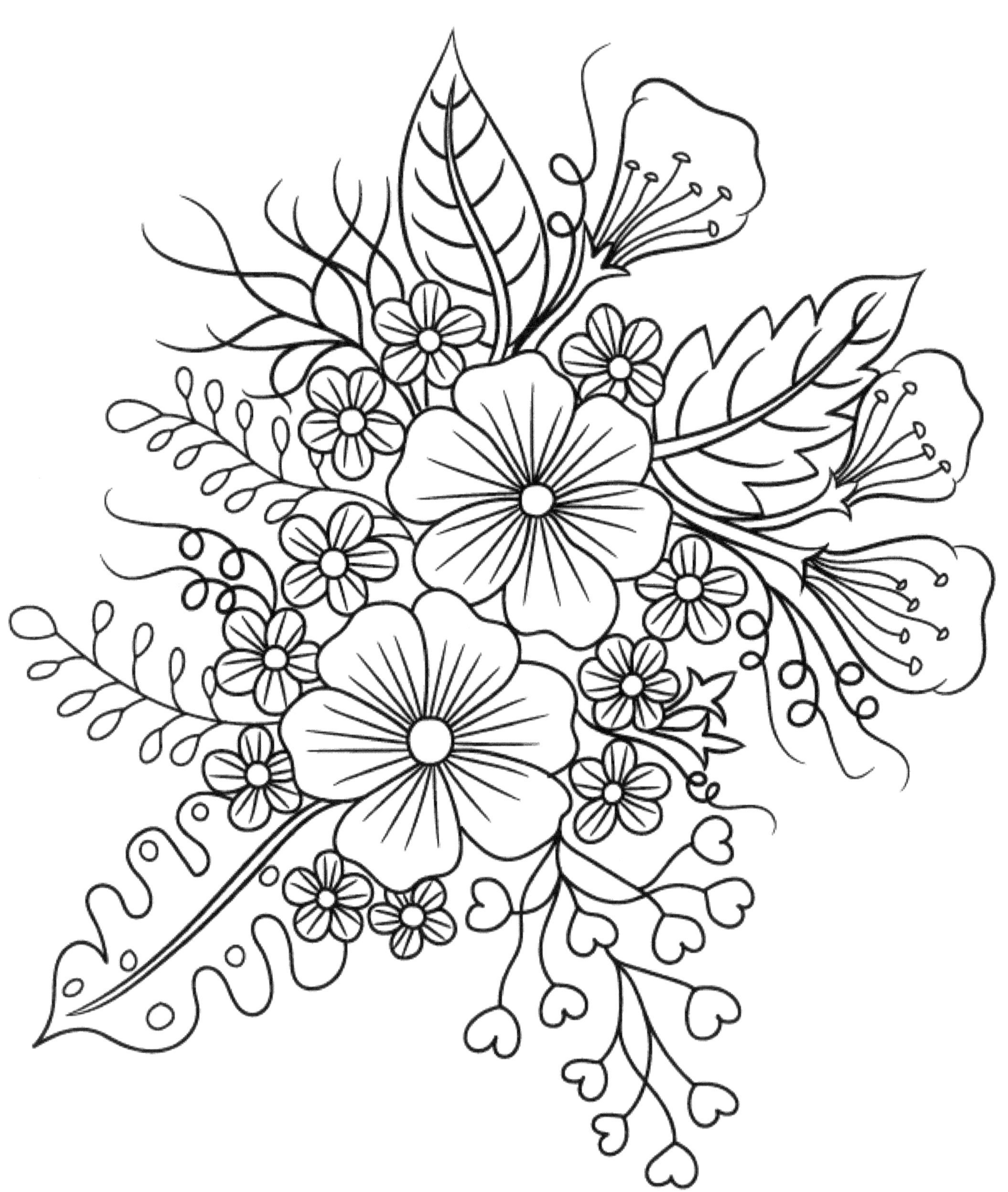

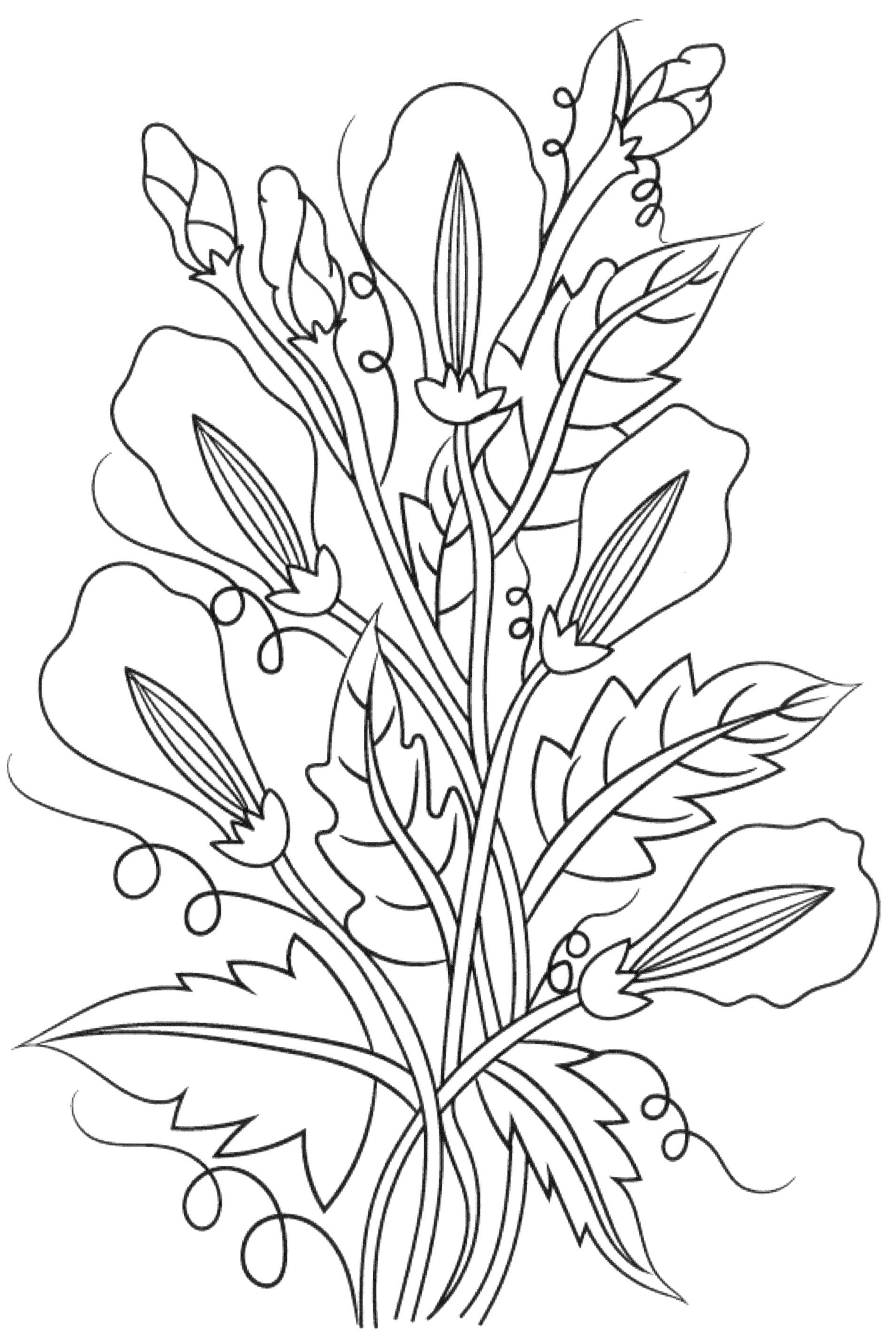

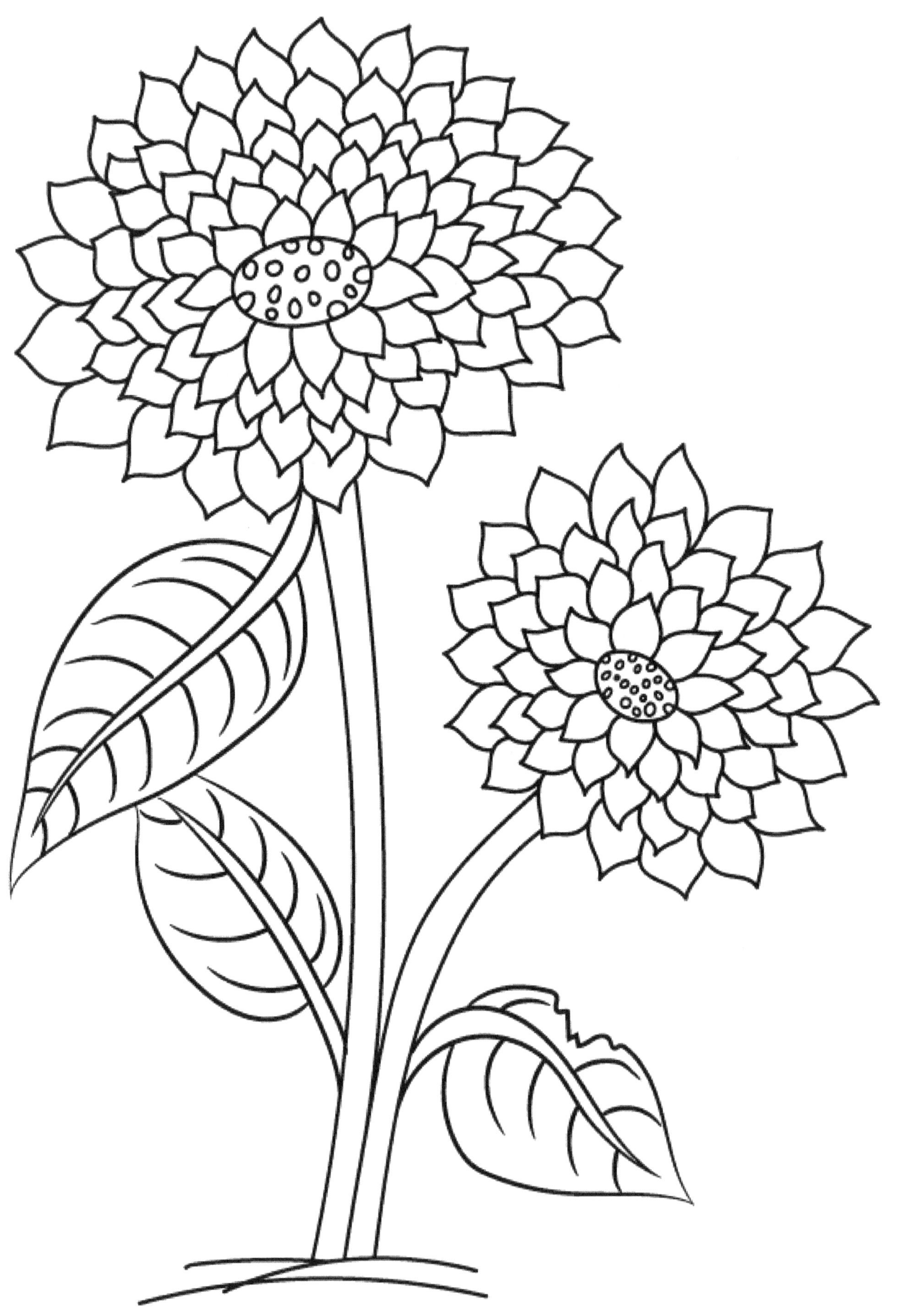

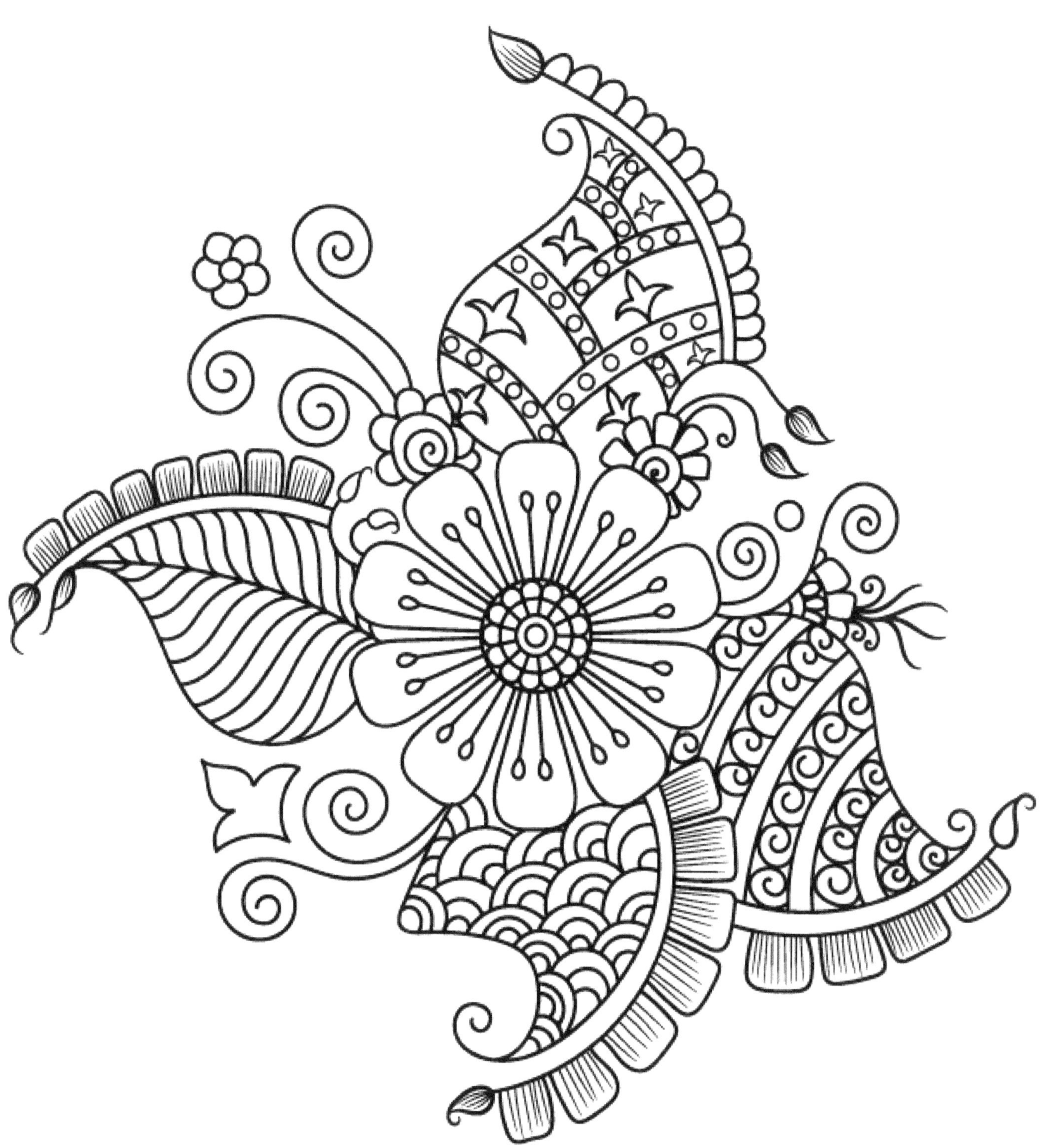

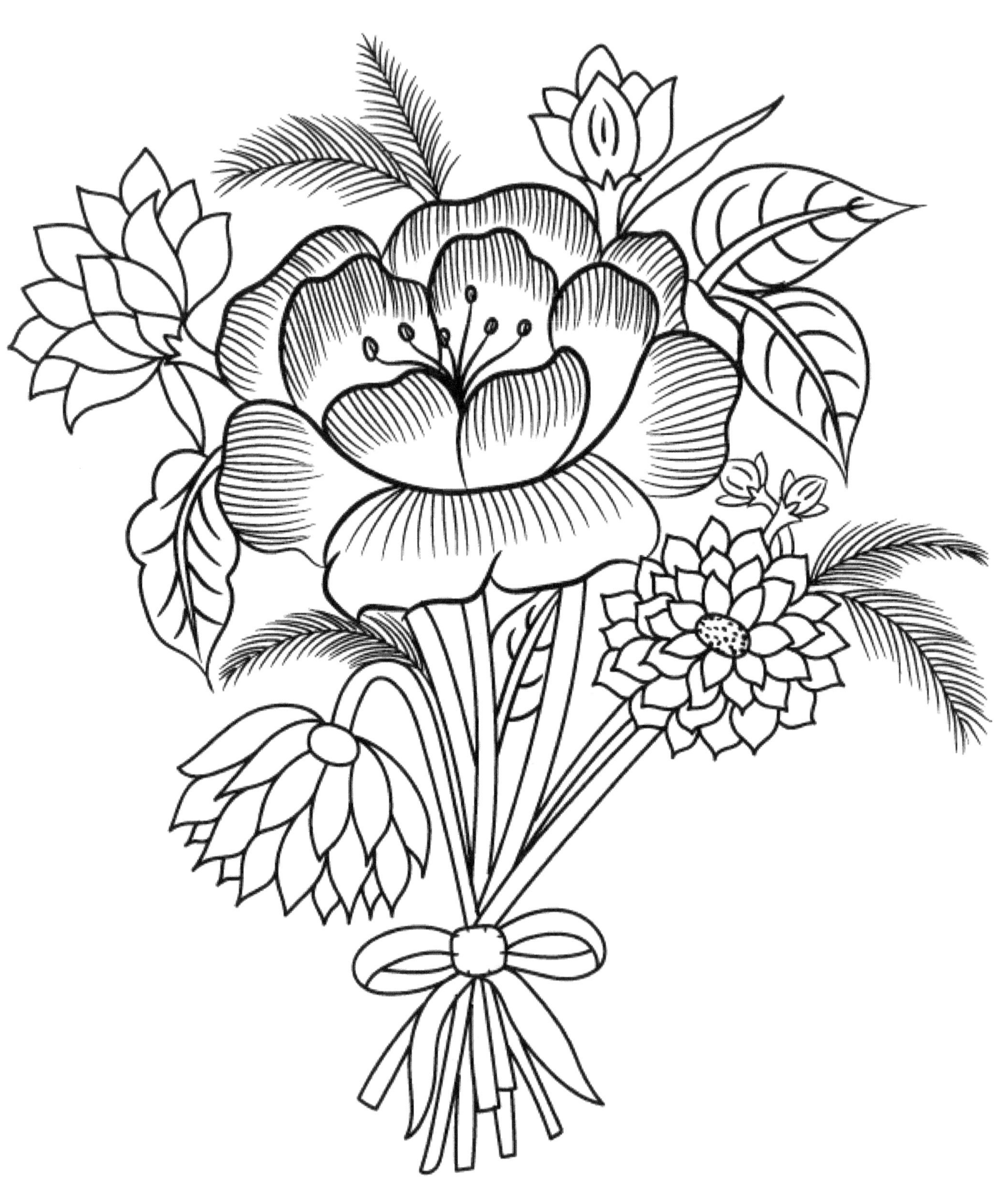

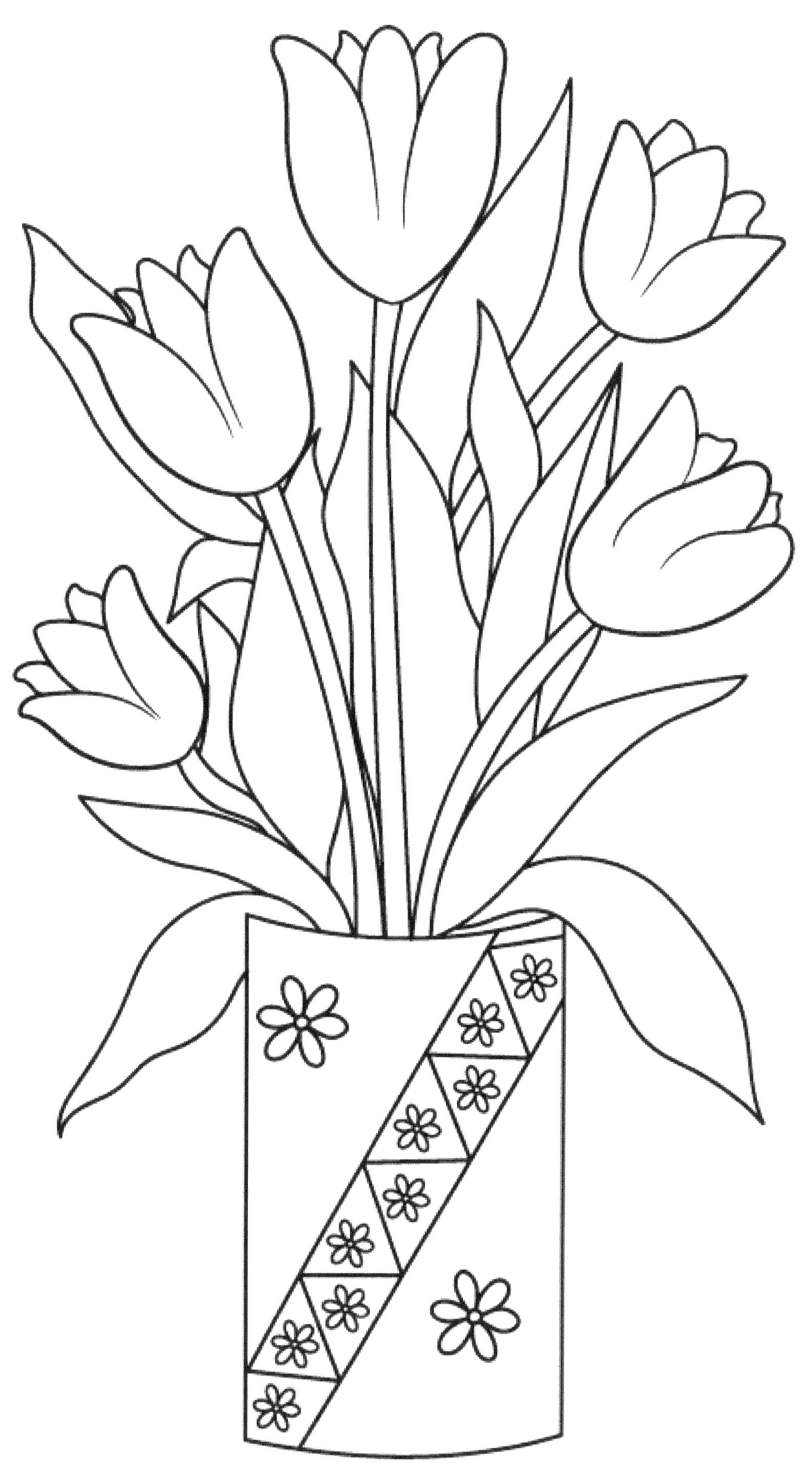

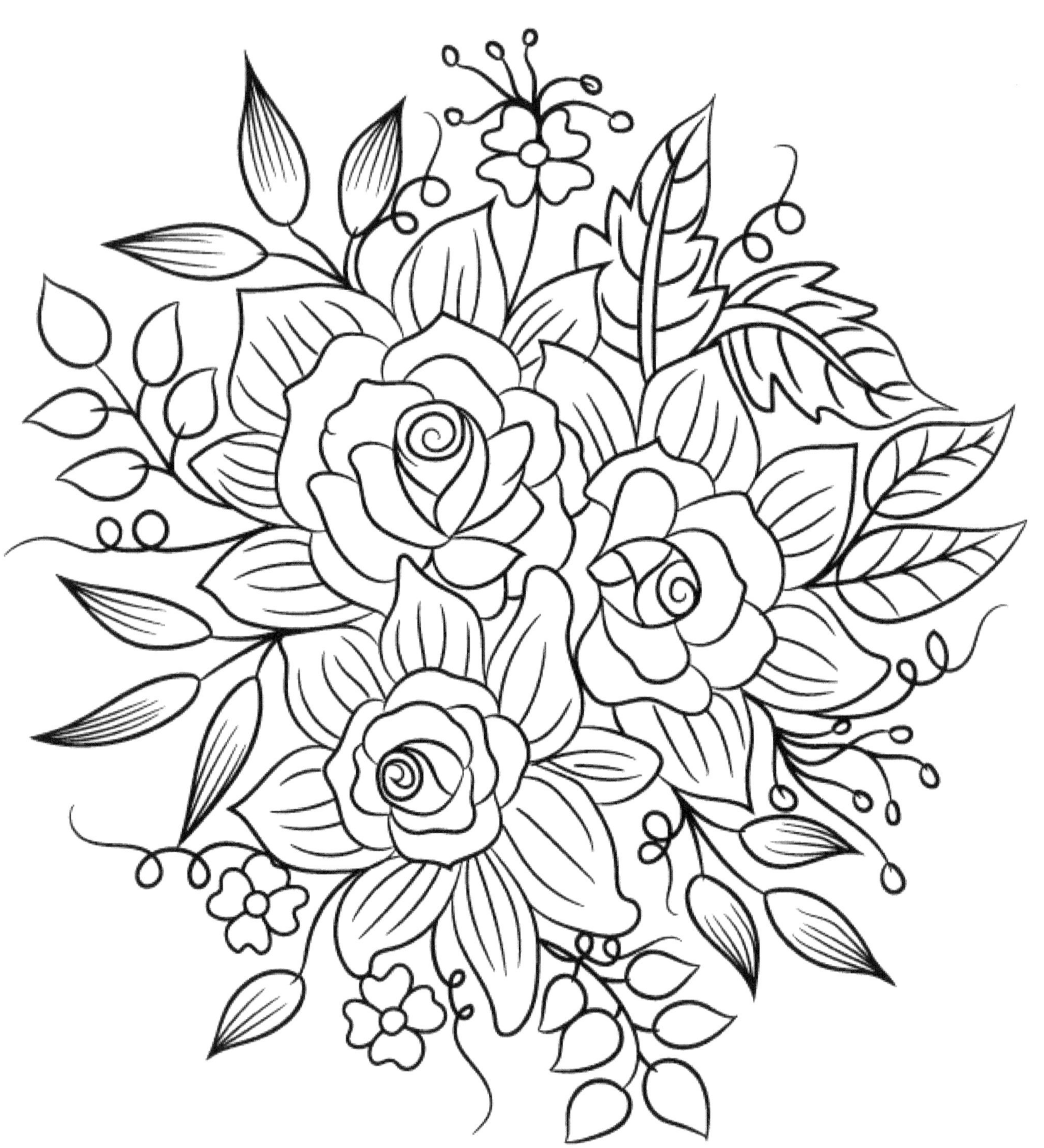

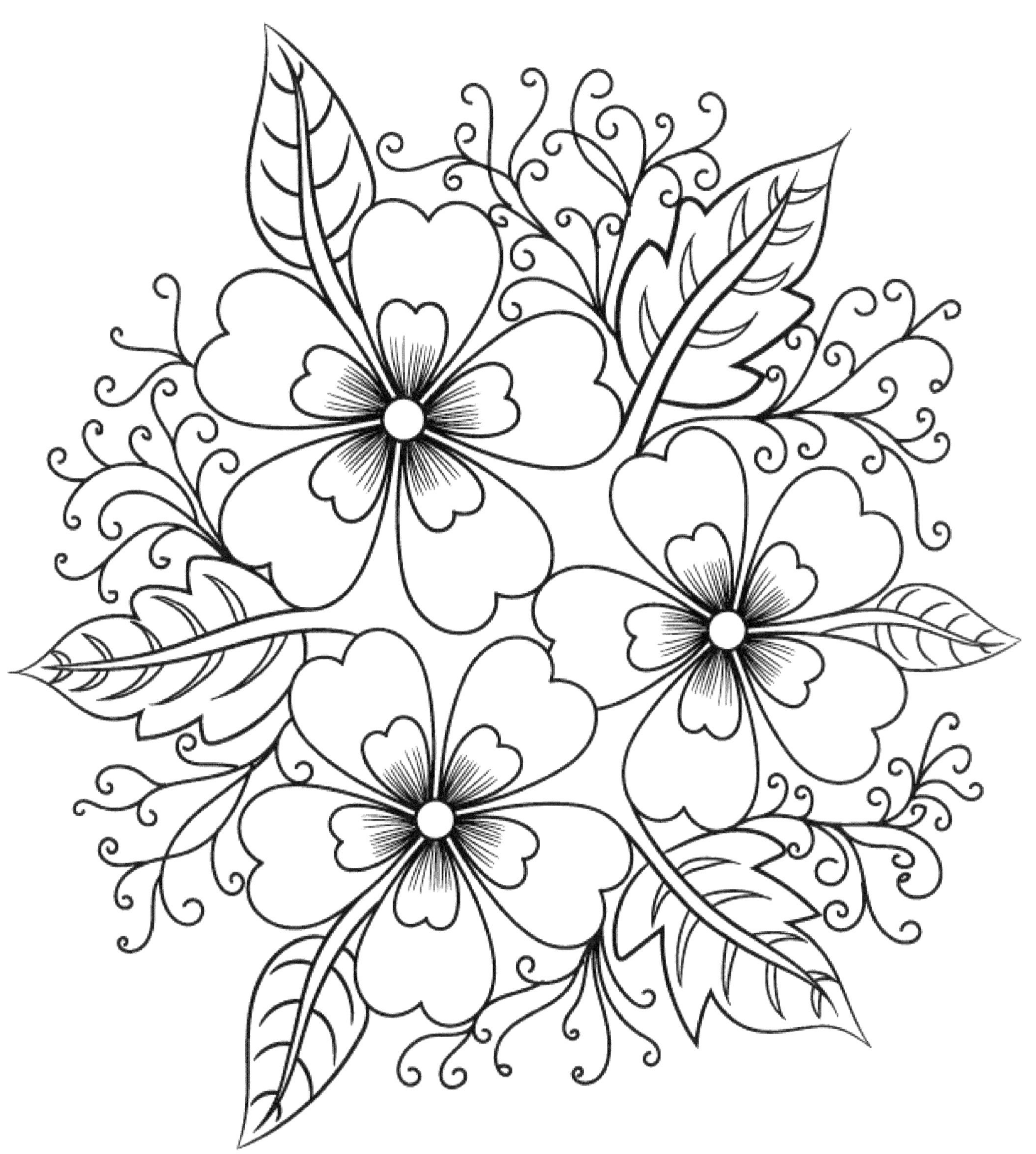

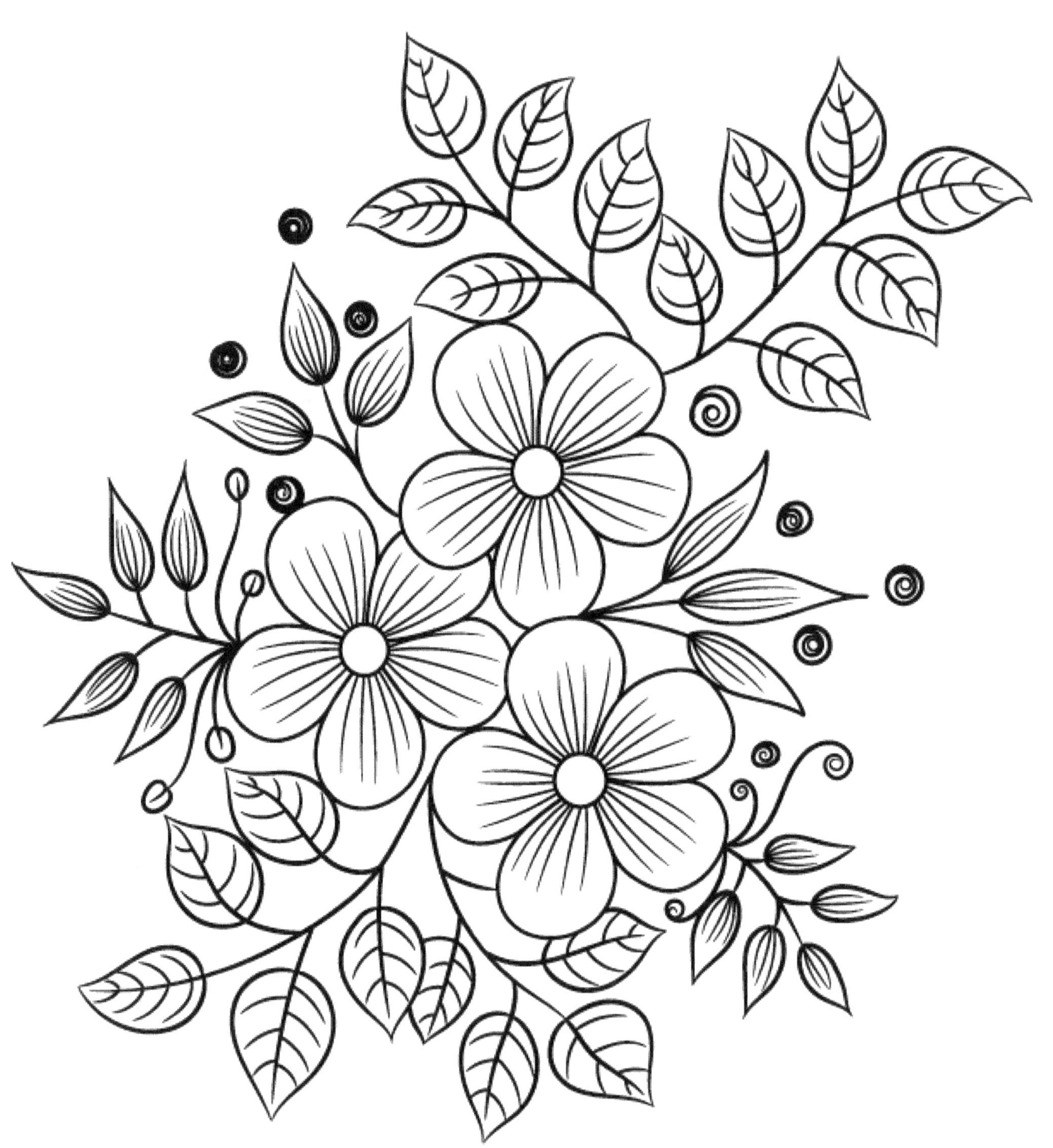

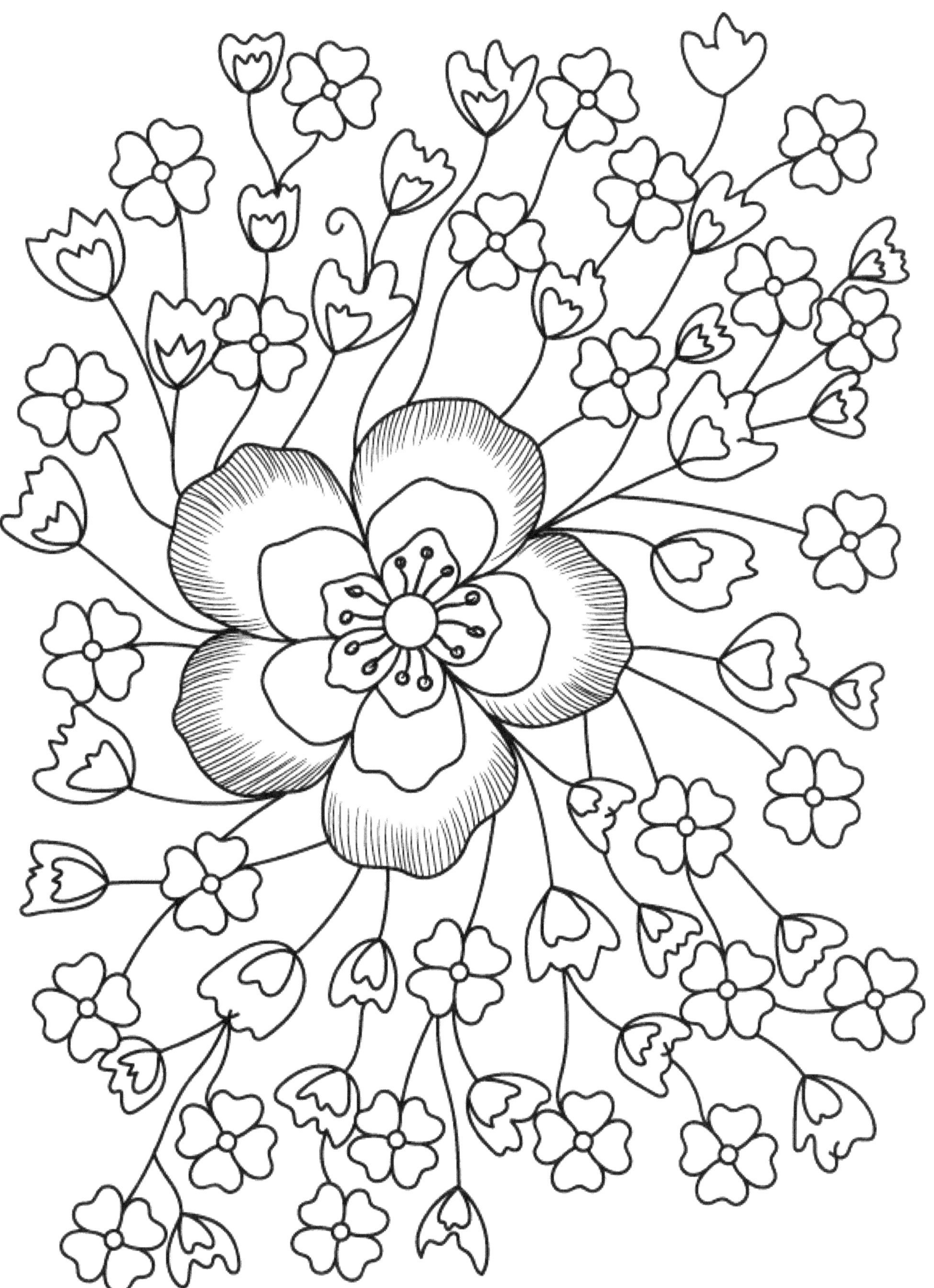

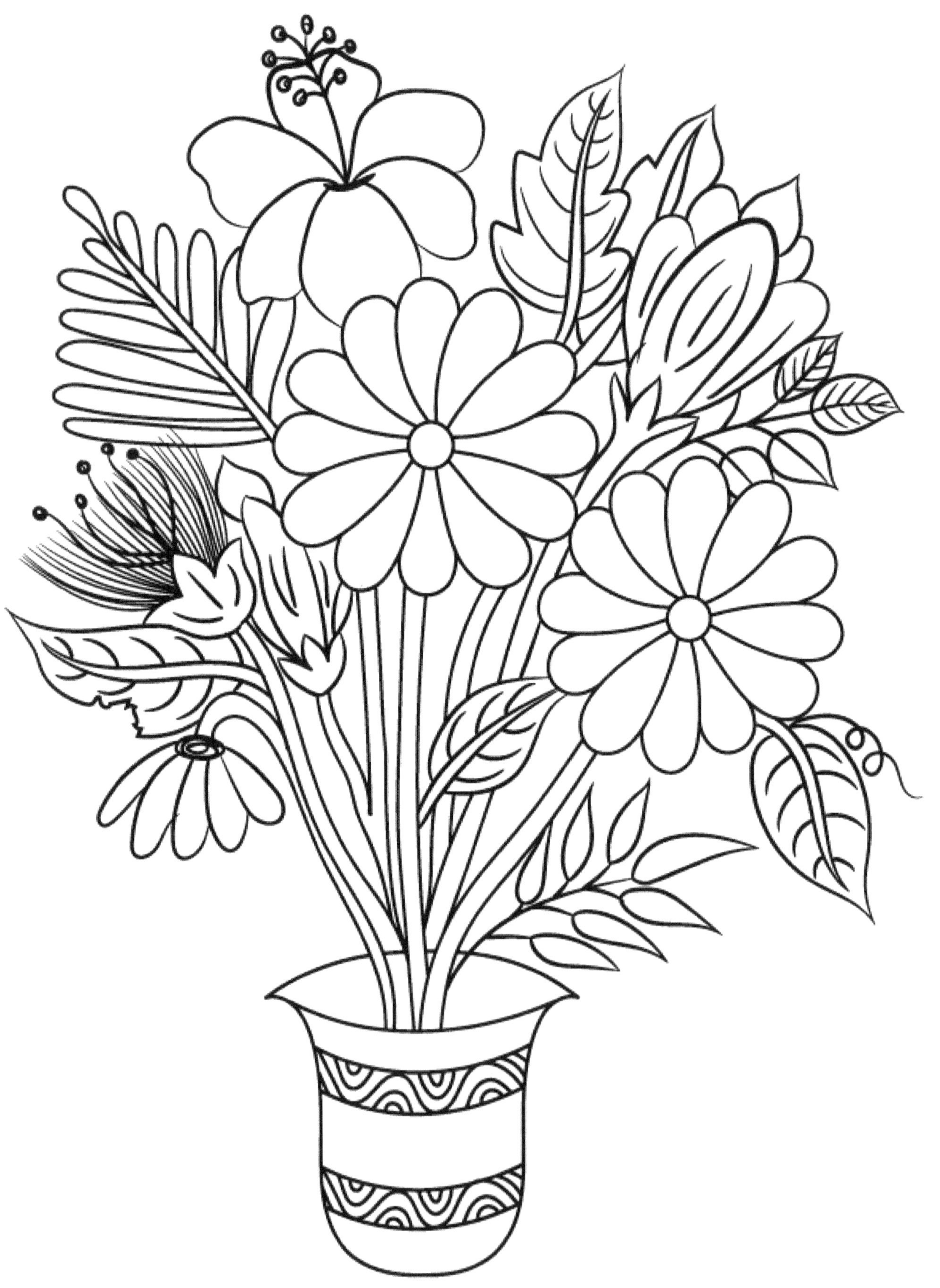

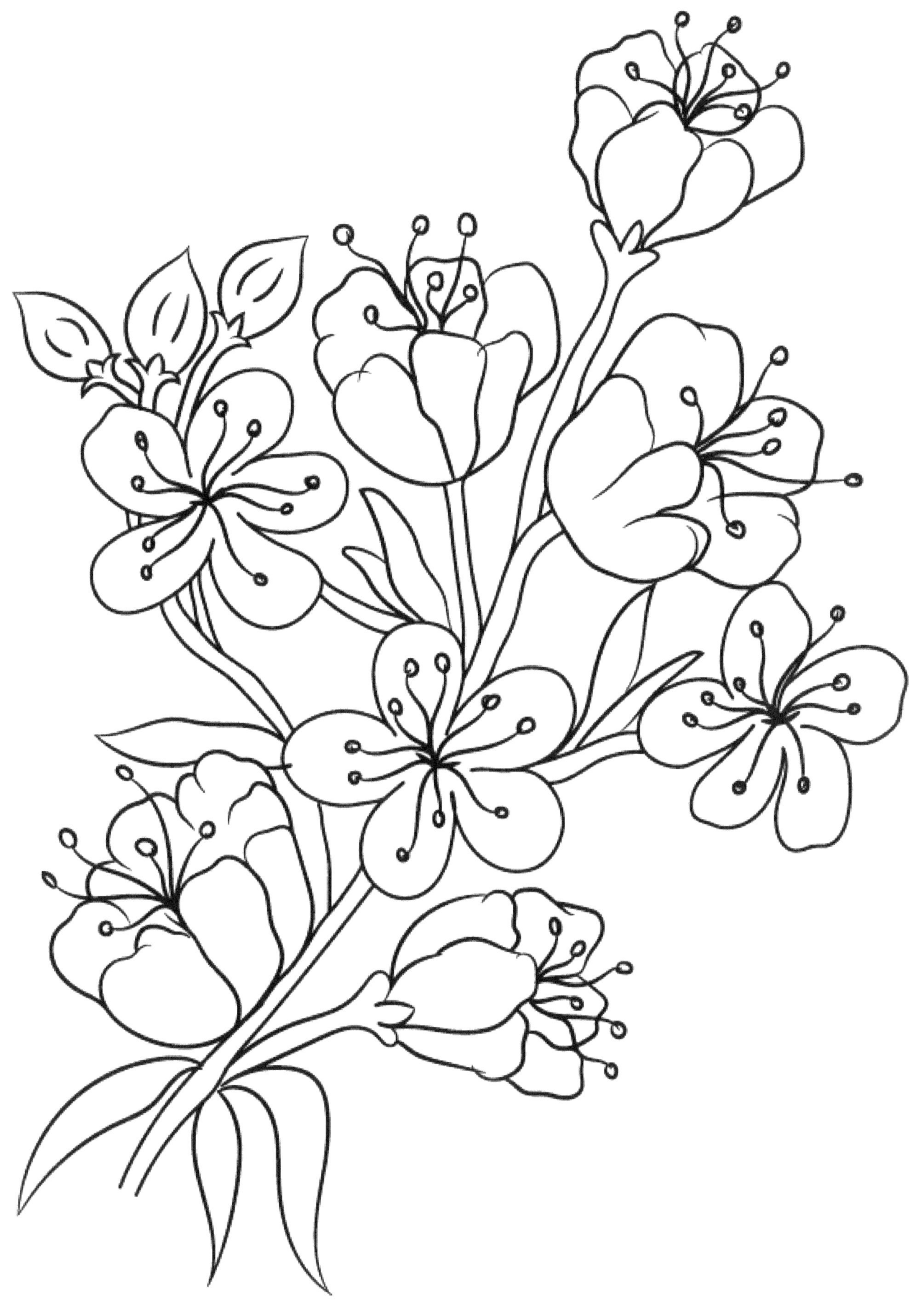

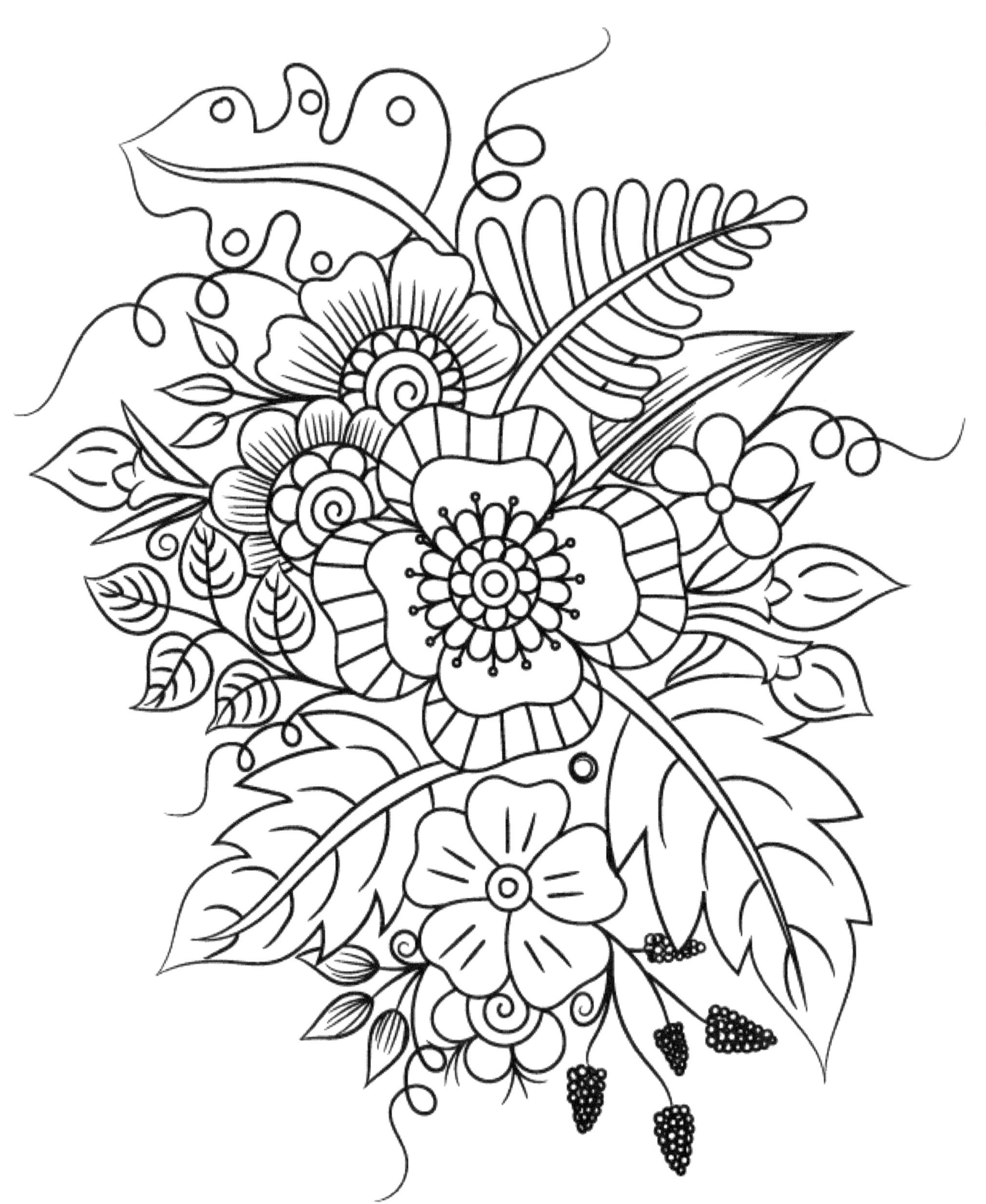

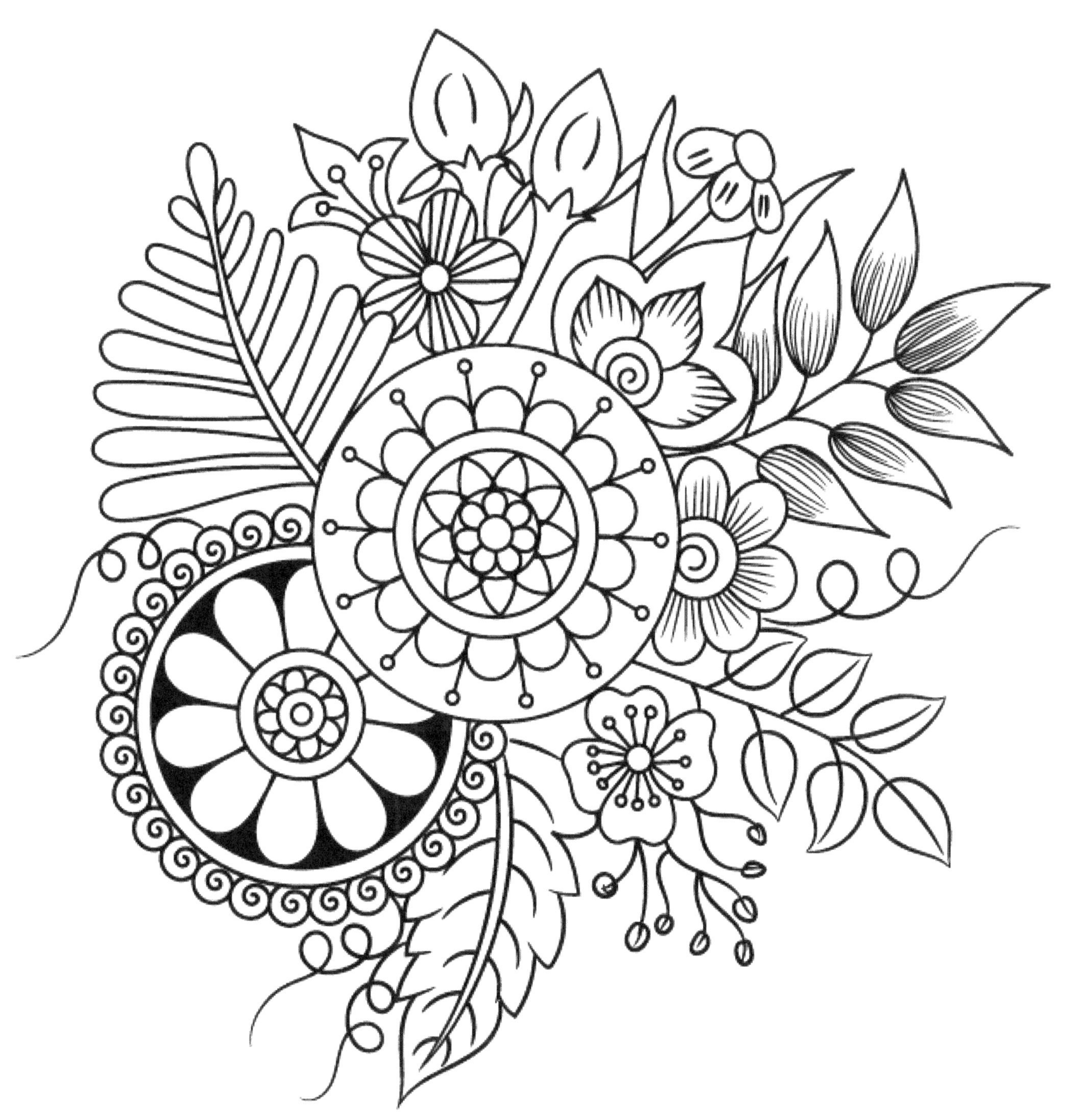

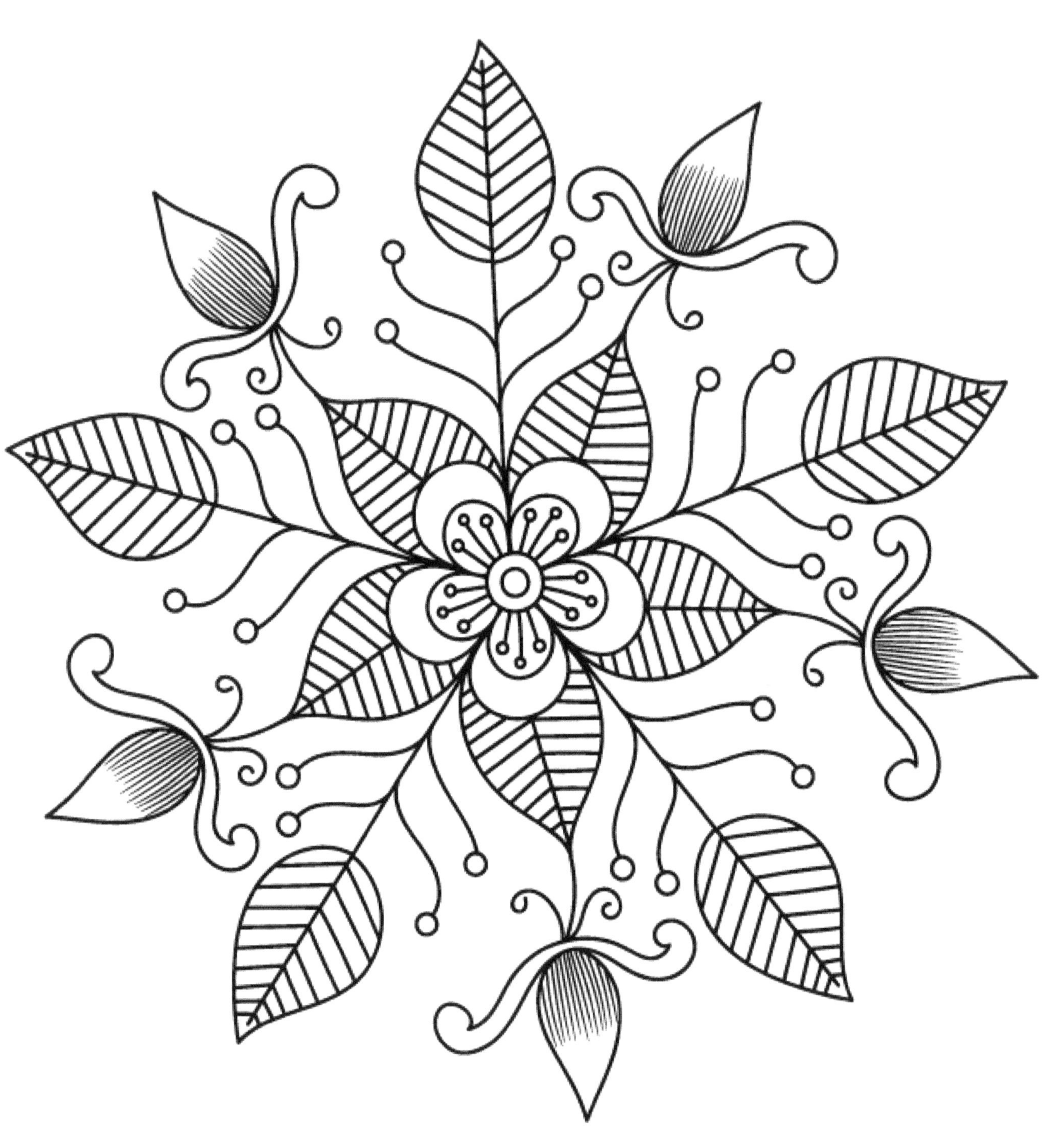

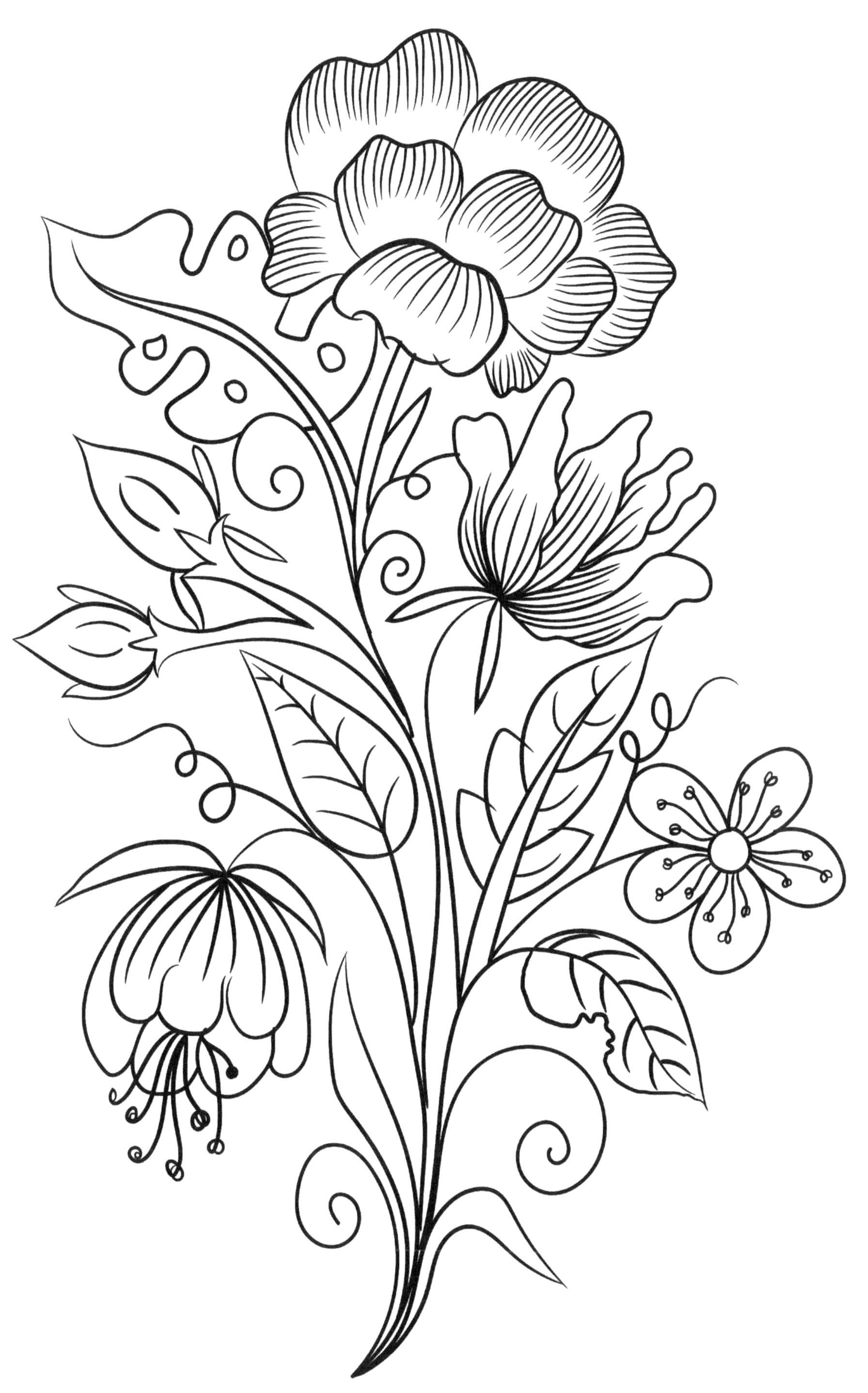

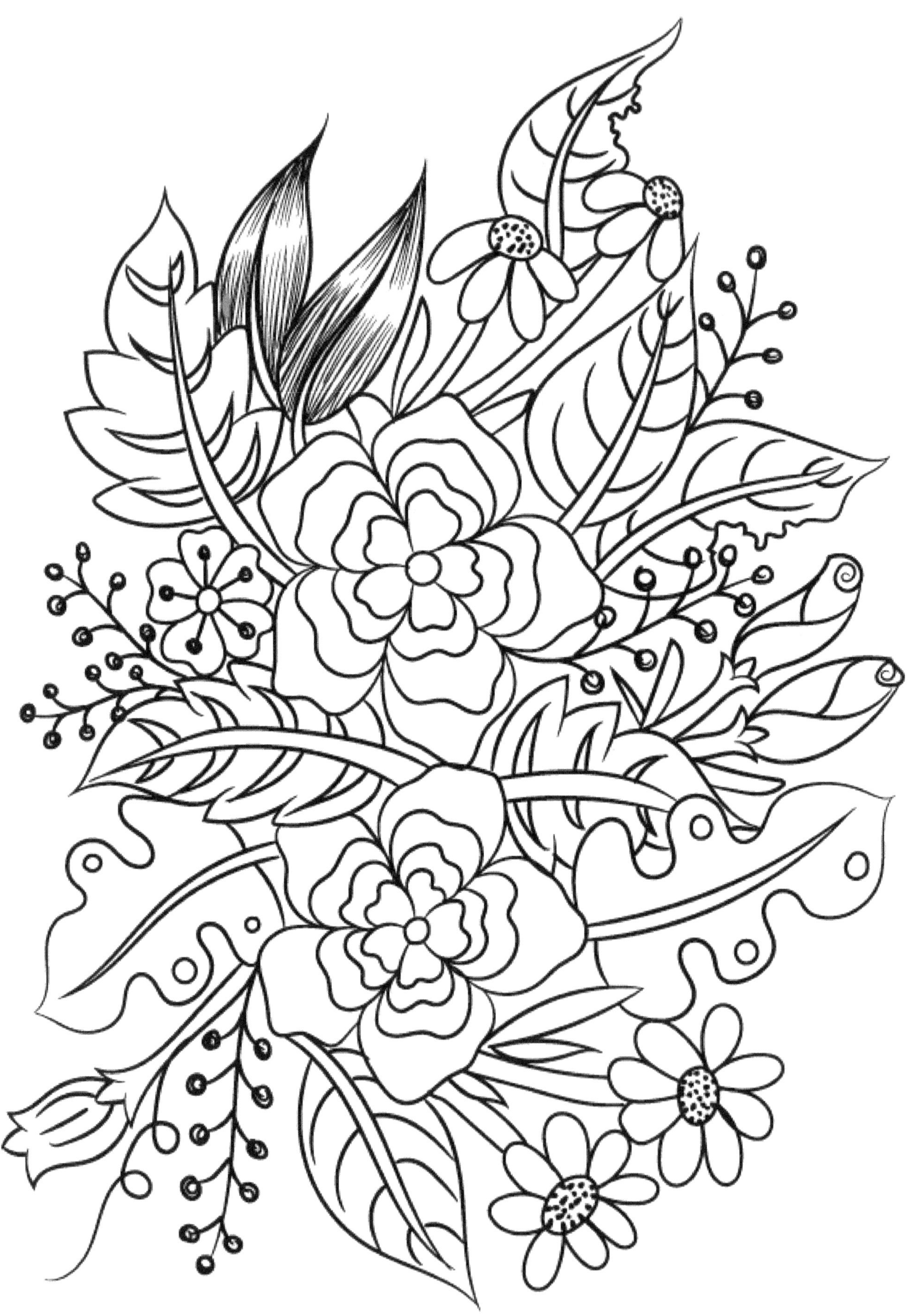

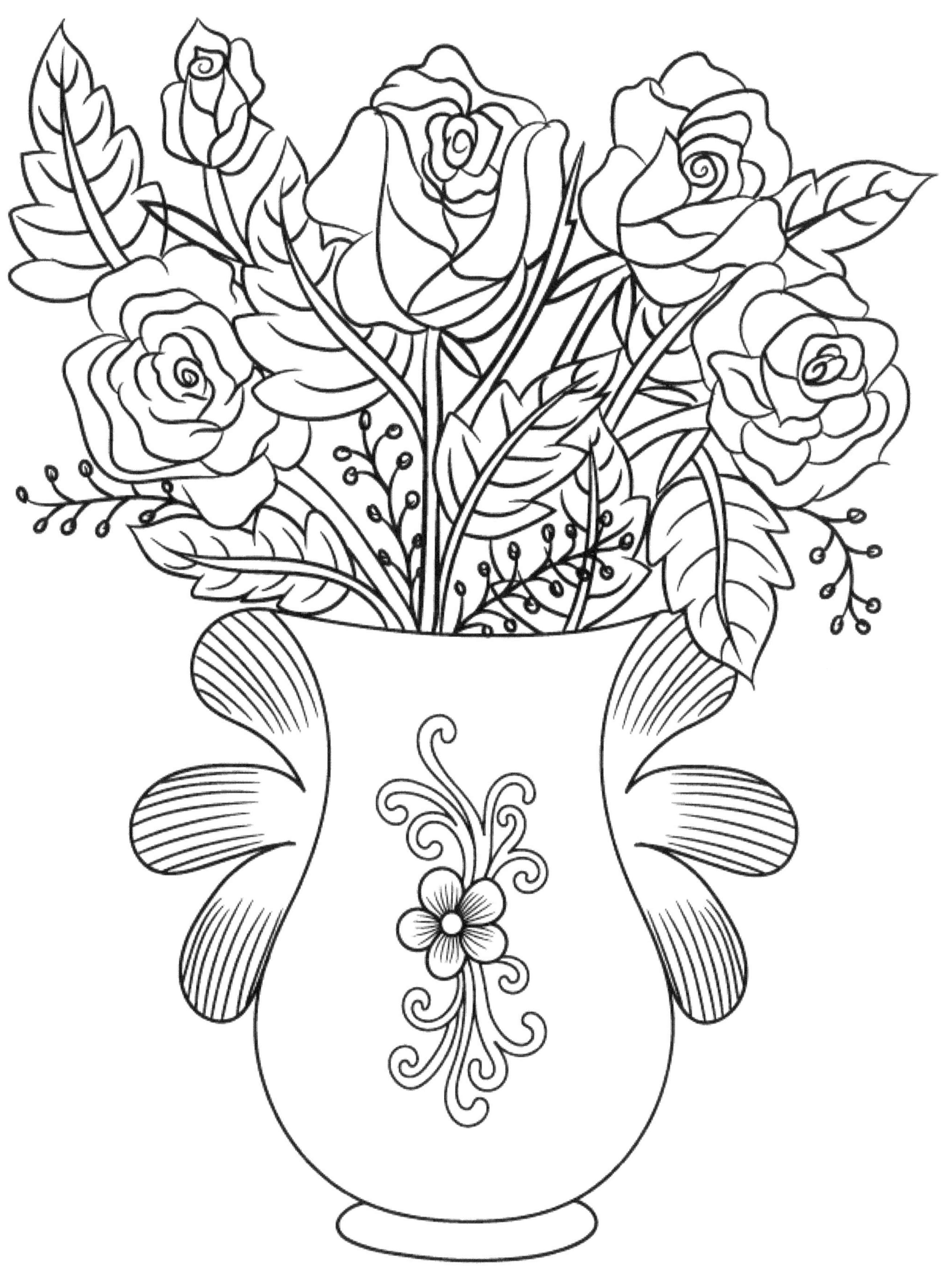

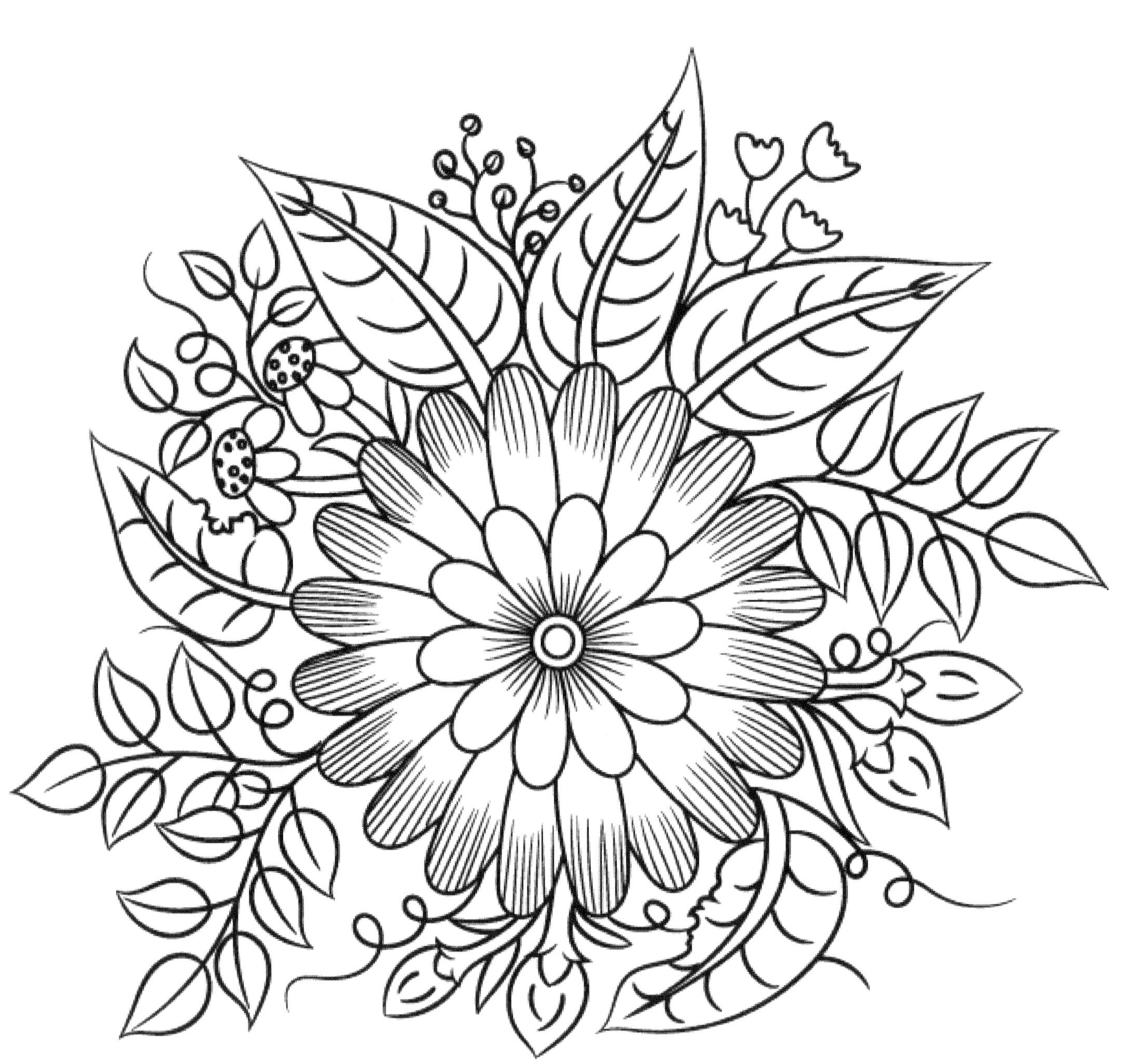

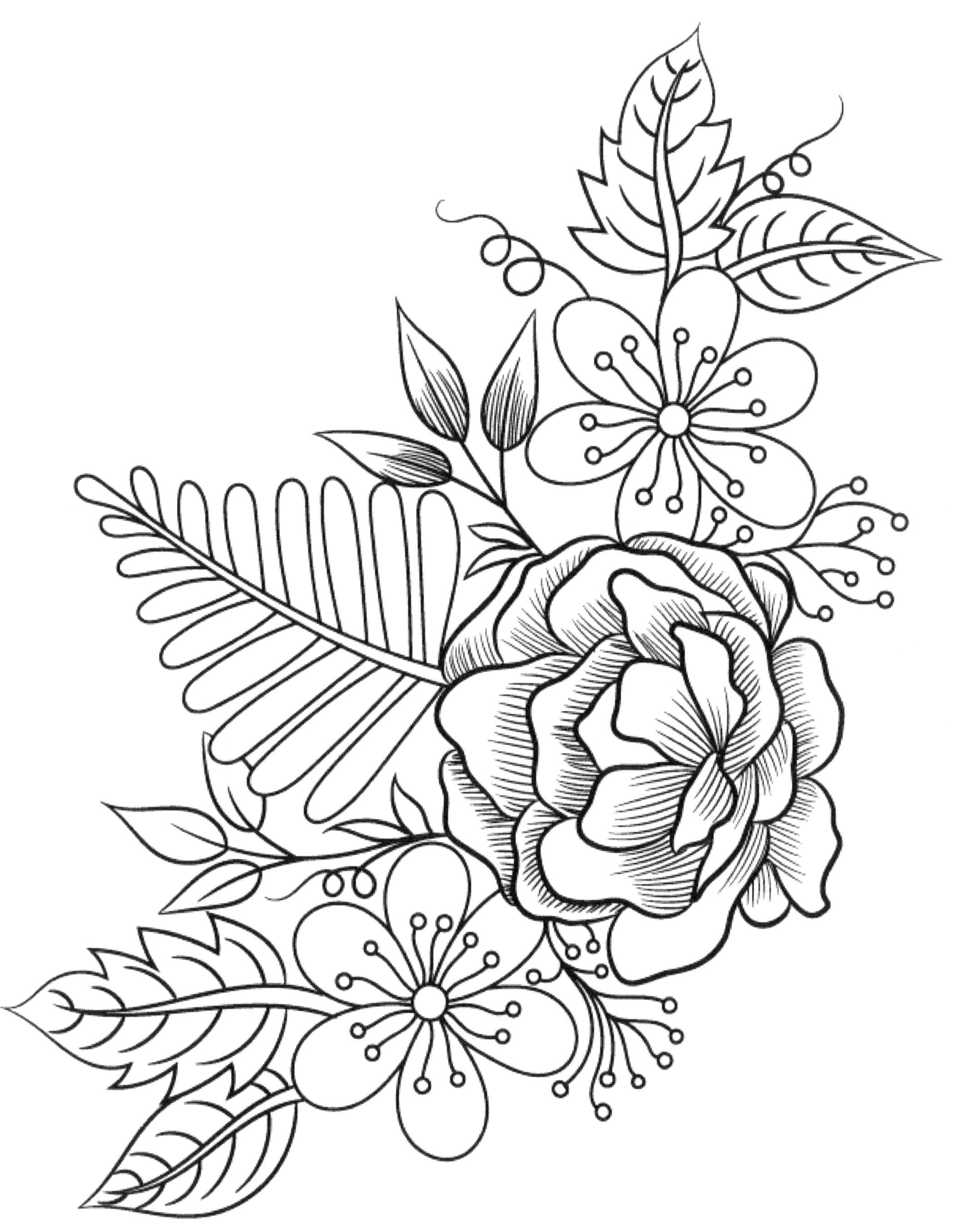

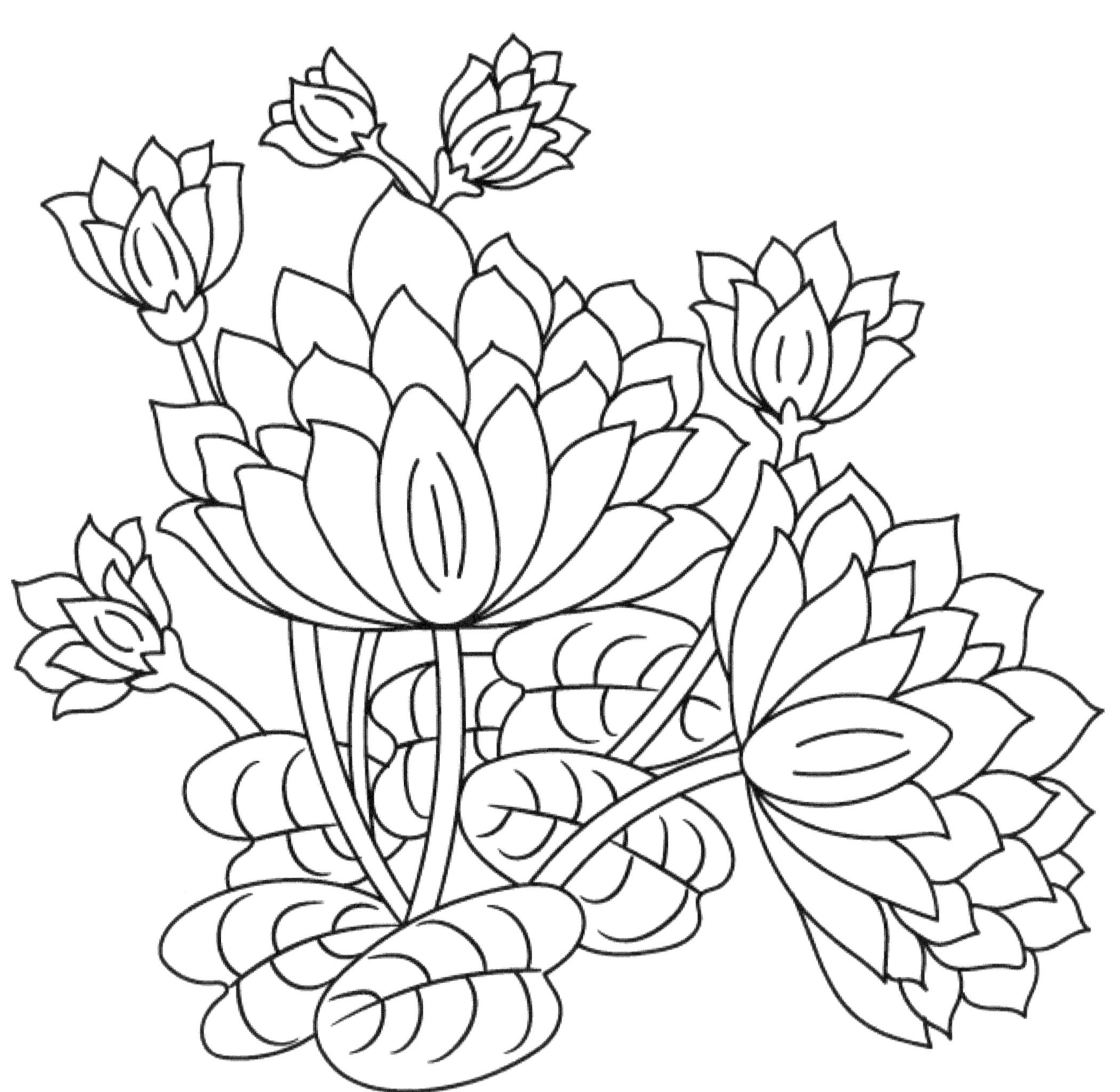

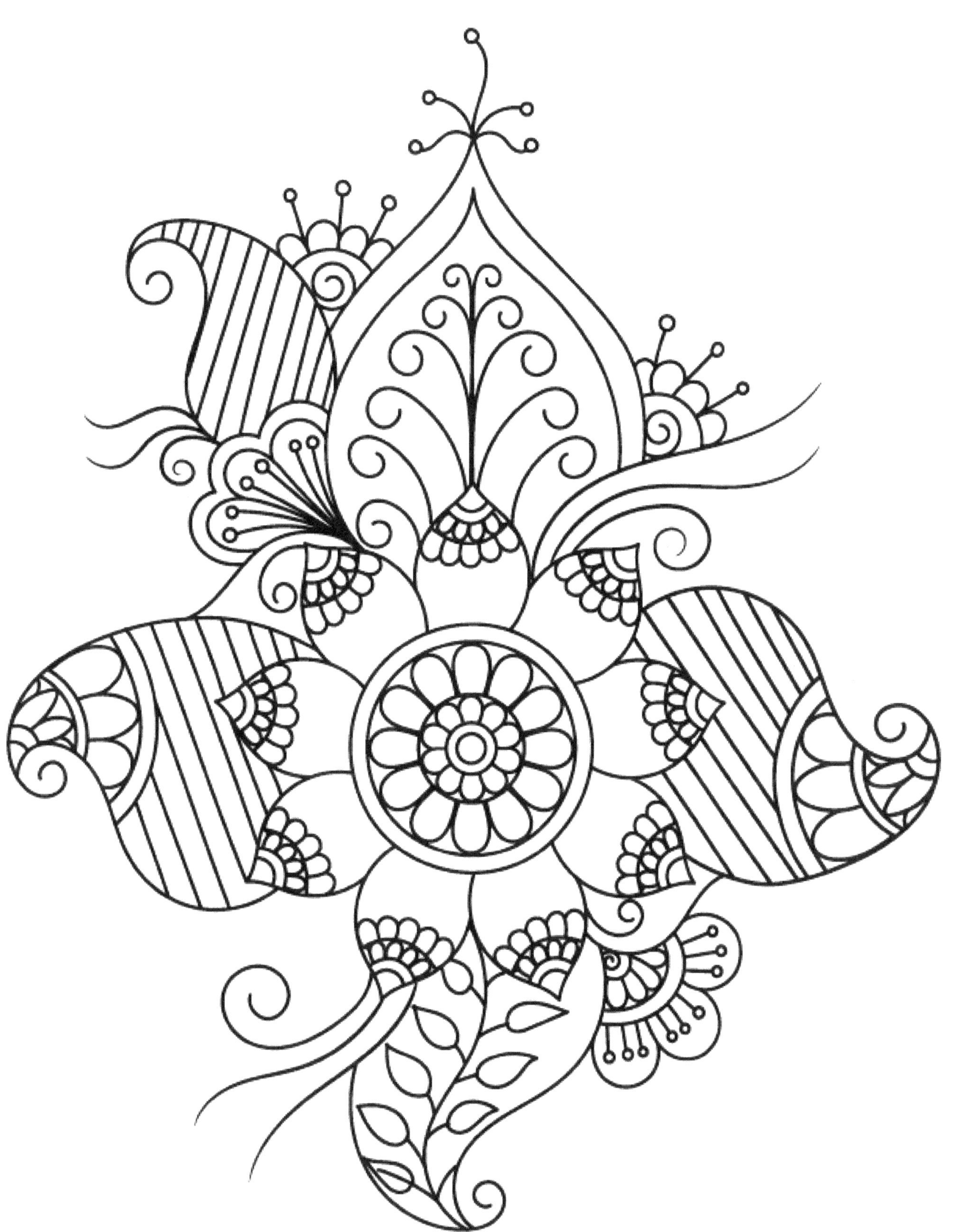

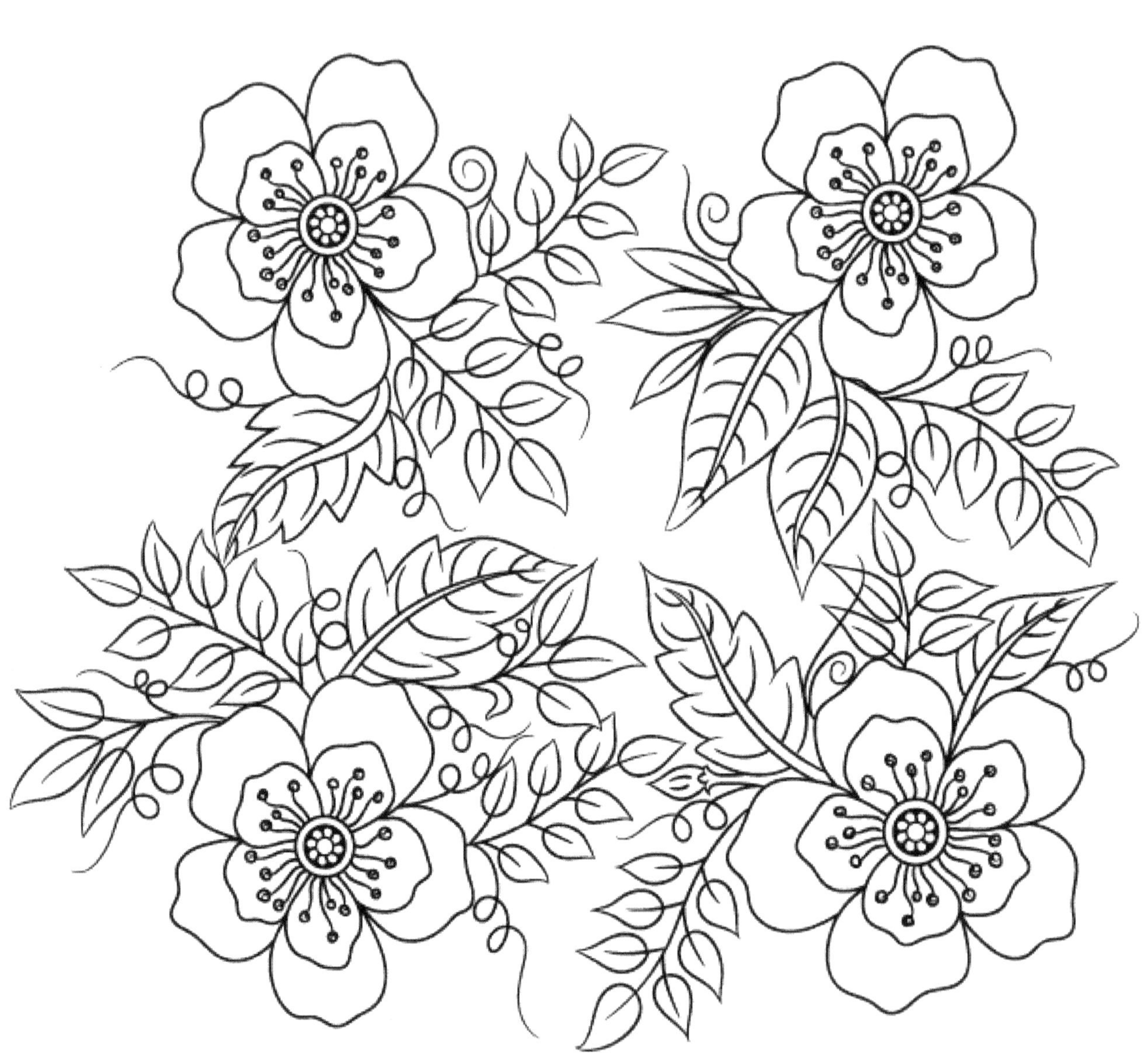

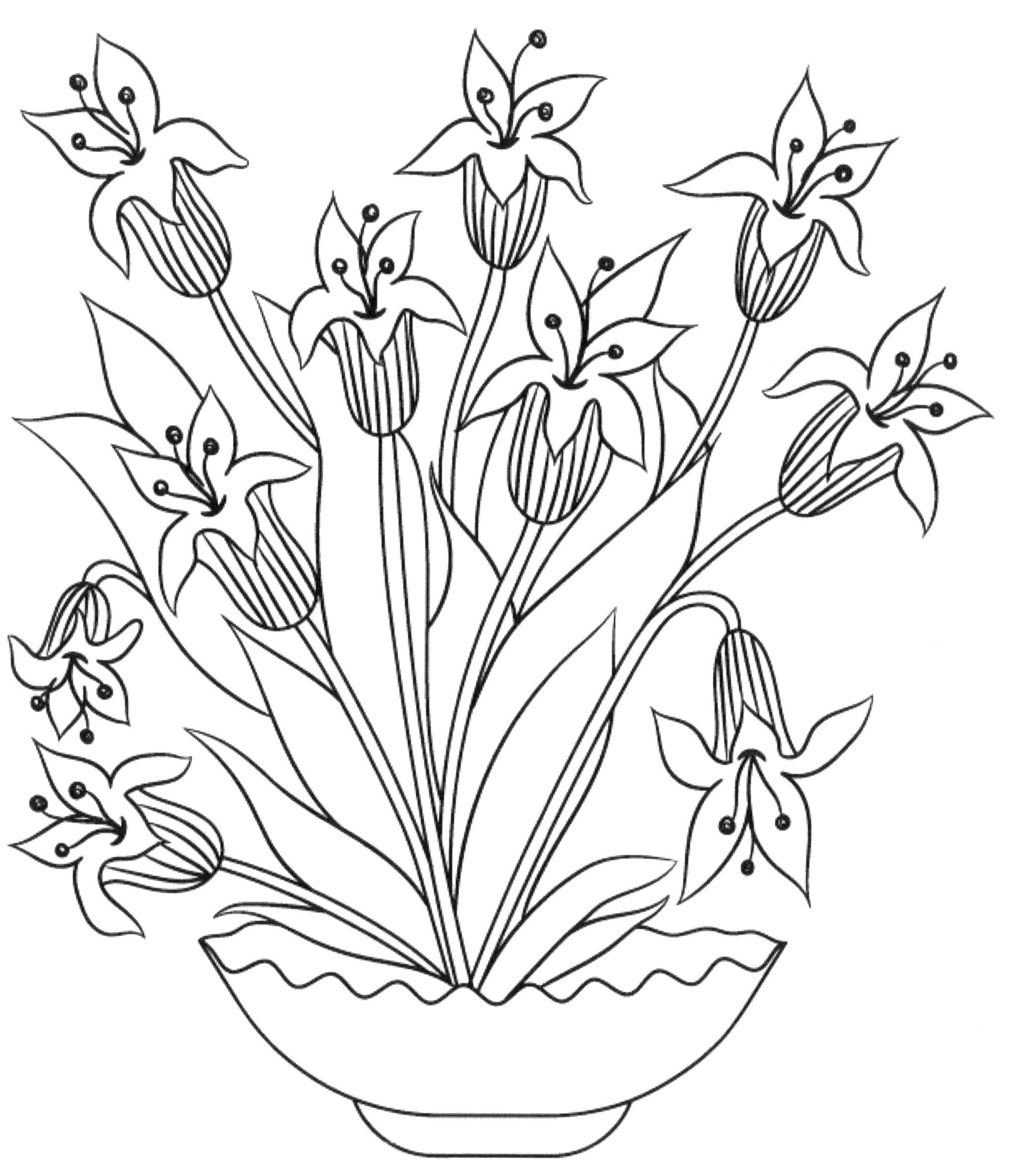

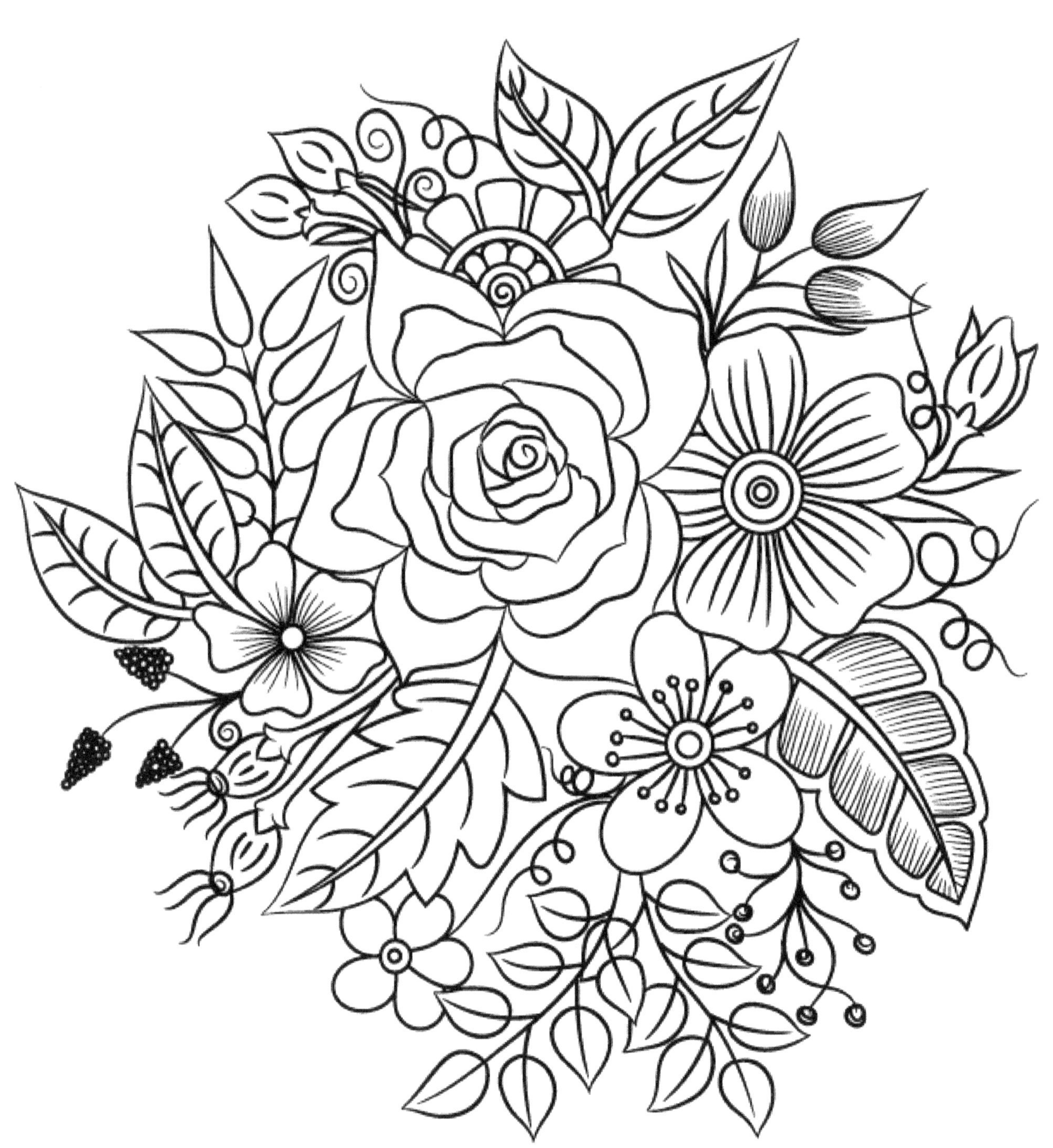

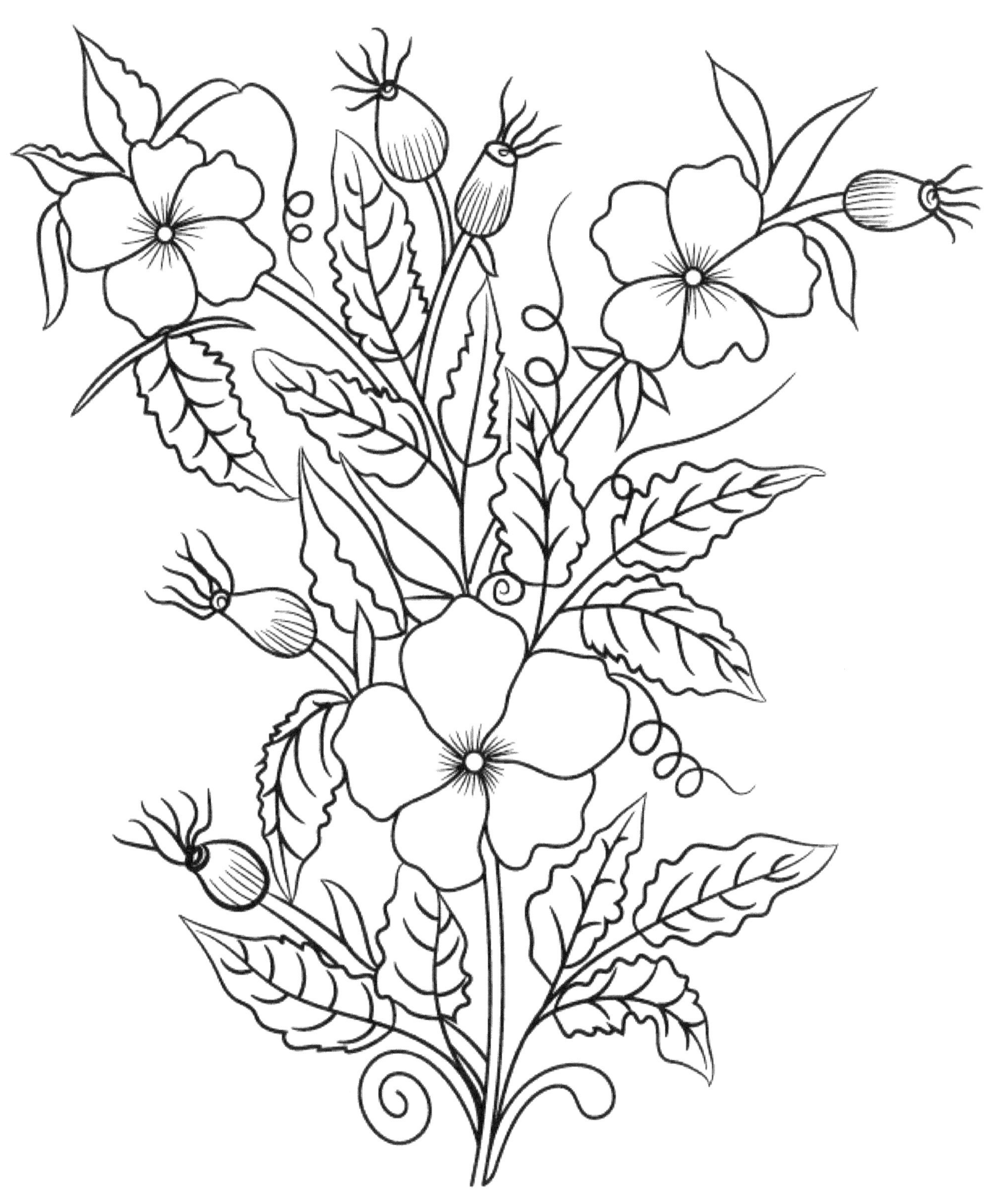

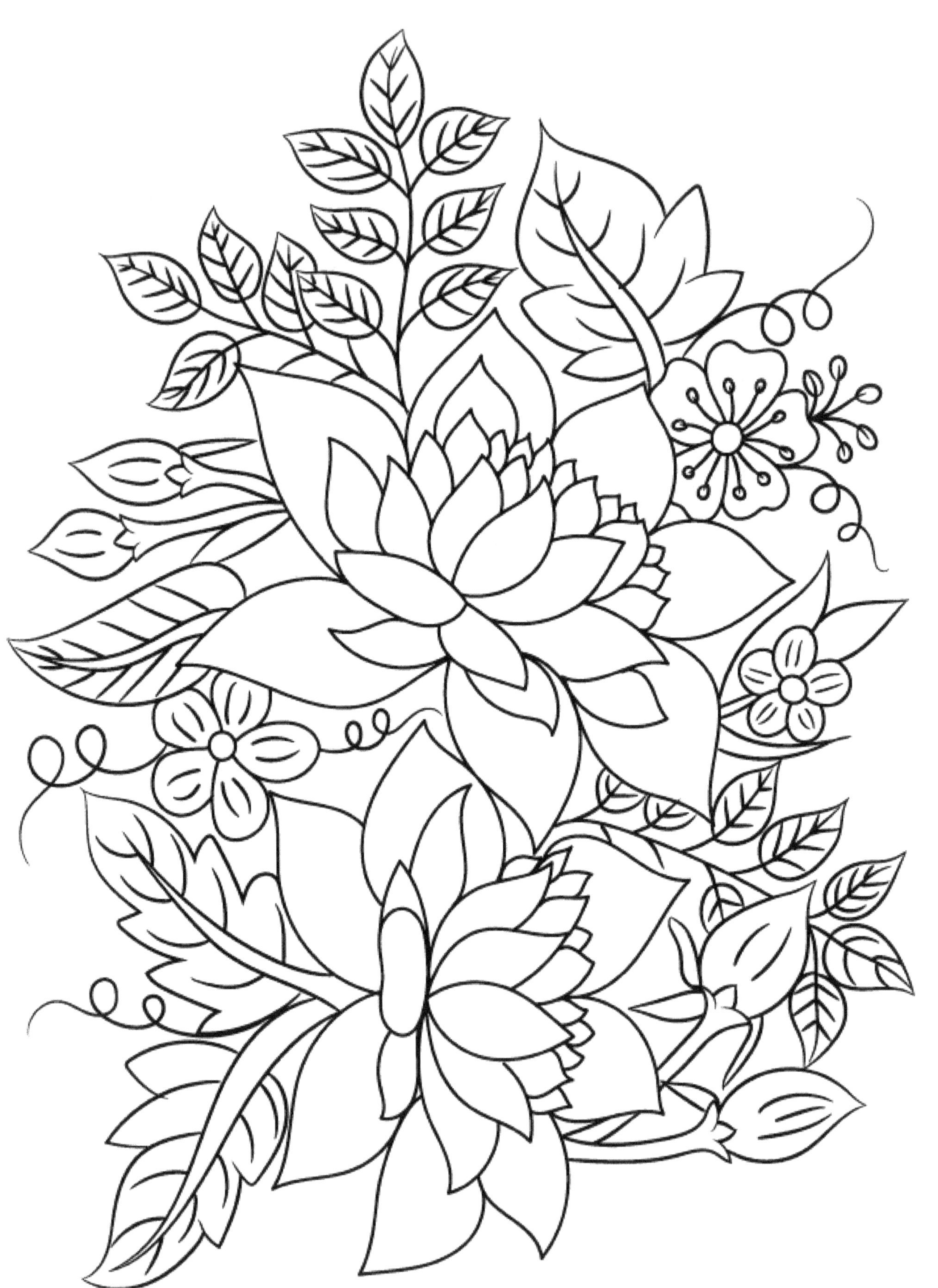

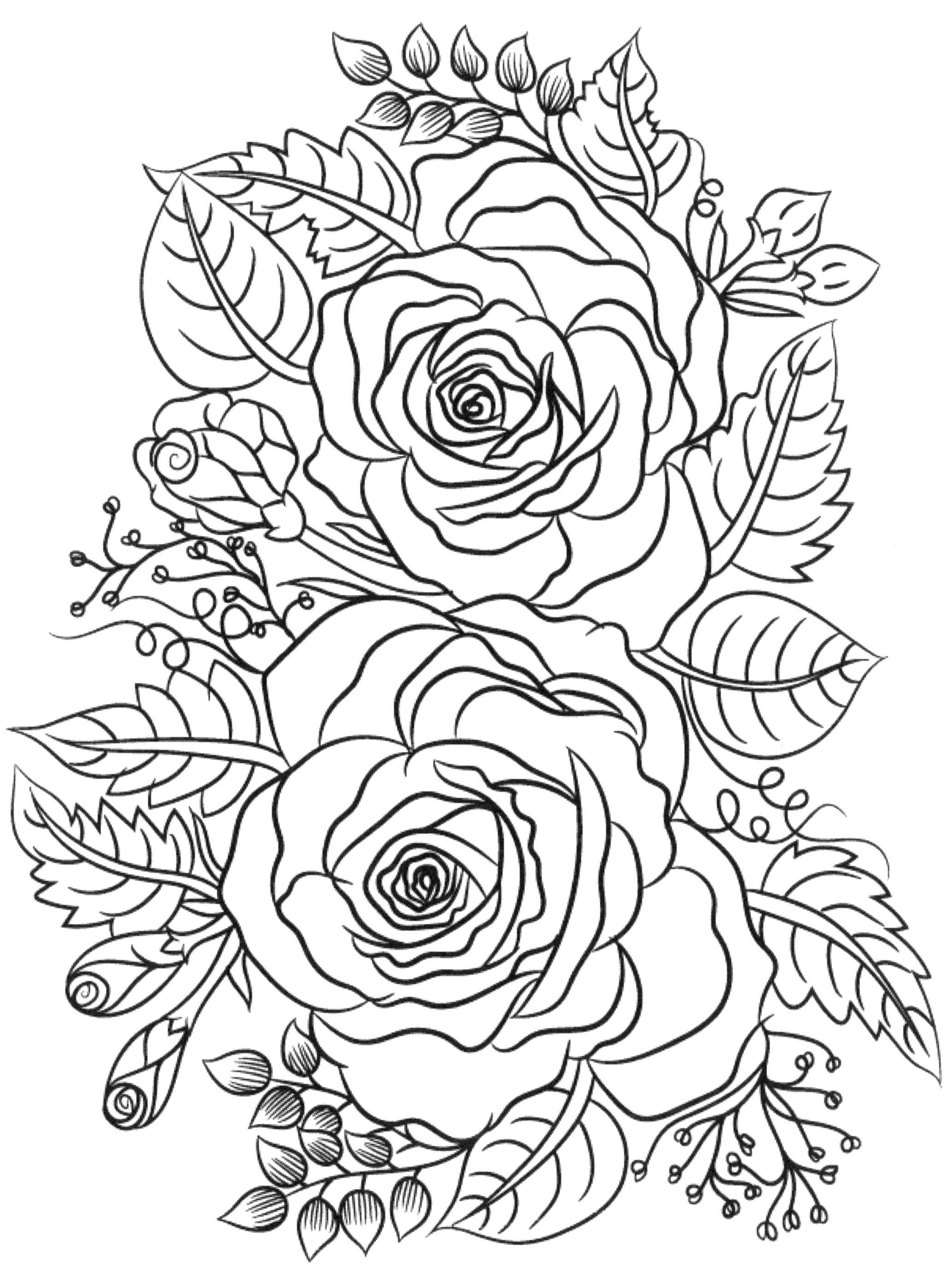

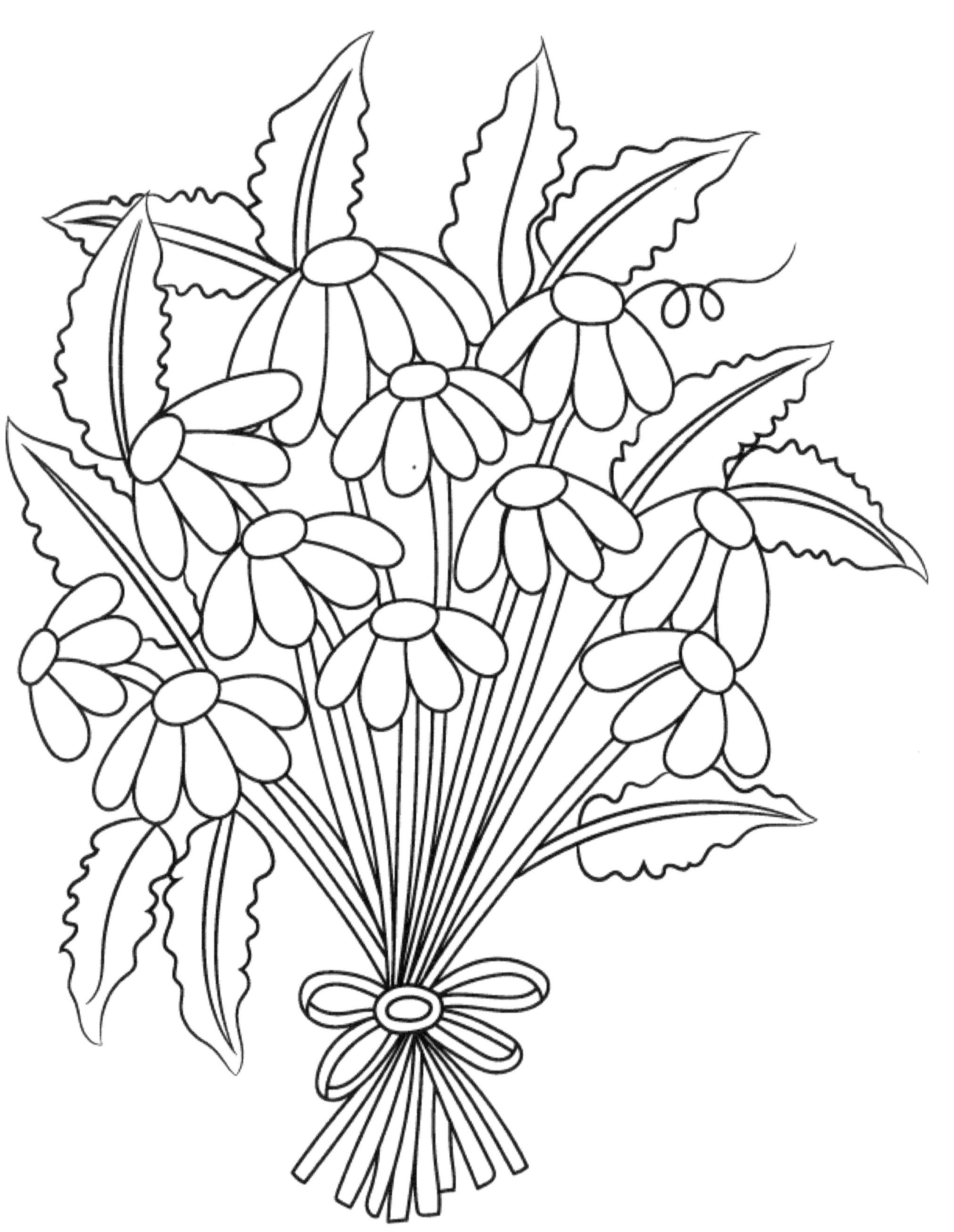

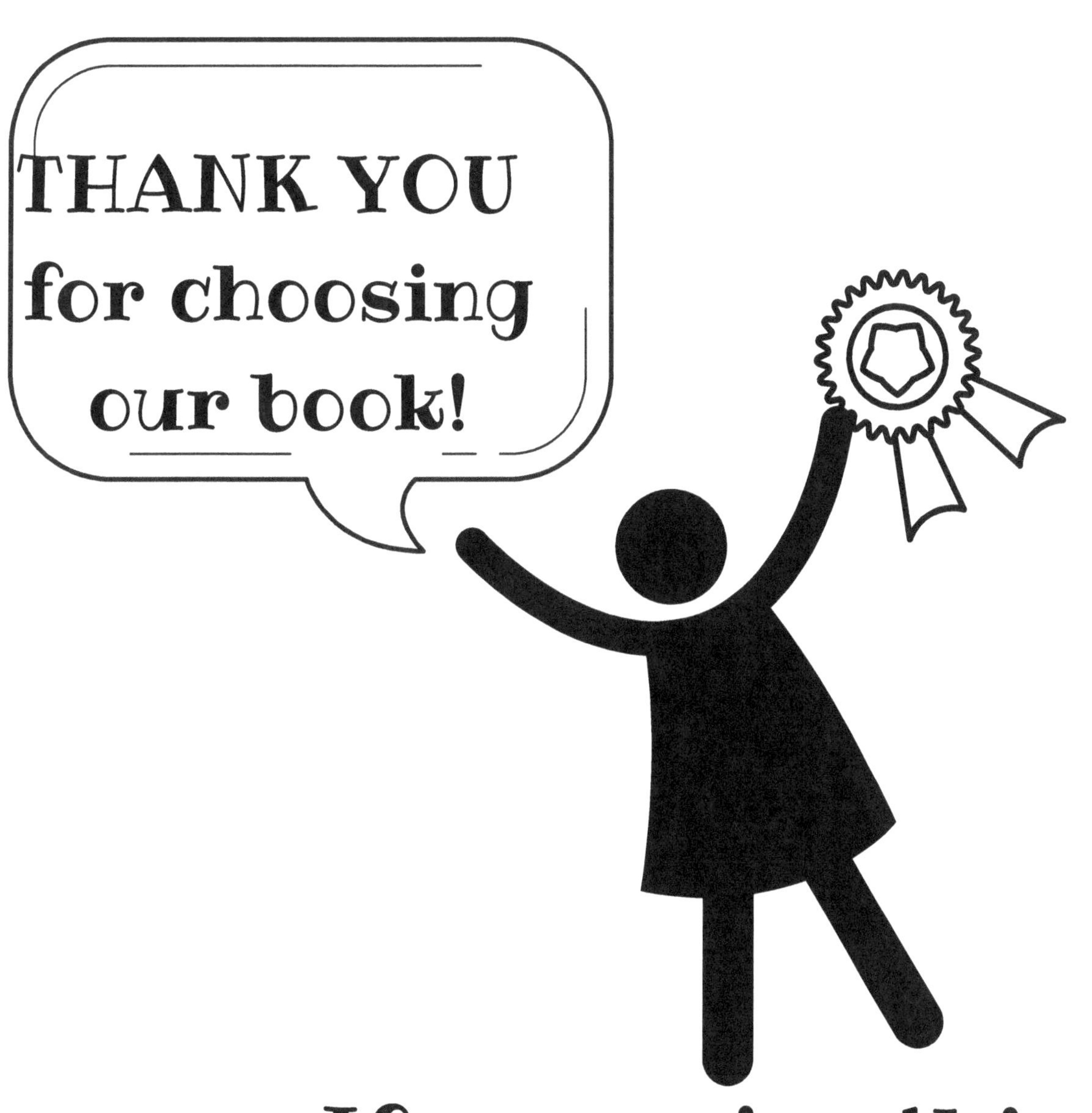

THANK YOU
for choosing
our book!

If you enjoy this
book at all, a quick
review on Amazon
would
really help us!